Anti-Movements
in America

This is a volume in the Arno Press series

Anti-Movements in America

Advisory Editor
Gerald N. Grob

Editorial Board
Ray Allen Billington
Nathan Glazer
Irving Louis Horowitz

*See last pages of this volume
for a complete list of titles.*

THE MELTING-POT MISTAKE

HENRY PRATT FAIRCHILD

ARNO PRESS

A New York Times Company

New York / 1977

ST. PHILIPS COLLEGE LIBRARY

Editorial Supervision: JOSEPH CELLINI

Reprint Edition 1977 by Arno Press Inc.

Reprinted from a copy in
The Newark Public Library

ANTI-MOVEMENTS IN AMERICA
ISBN for complete set: 0-405-09937-1
See last pages of this volume for titles.

Manufactured in the United States of America

Library of Congress Cataloging in Publication Data

Fairchild, Henry Pratt, 1880-1956.
   The melting-pot mistake.

    (Anti-movements in America)
   Reprint of the 1926 ed. published by Little, Brown,
Boston.
   1. United States--Emigration and immigration.
2. United States--Foreign population. 3. Americaniza-
tion. I. Title. II. Series.
JV6465.F35   1977   325.73   76-46076
ISBN 0-405-09949-5

THE MELTING-POT MISTAKE

By
HENRY PRATT FAIRCHILD

BOSTON
LITTLE, BROWN, AND COMPANY
1926

Copyright, 1926,
BY HENRY PRATT FAIRCHILD.

All rights reserved

Published January, 1926

PRINTED IN THE UNITED STATES OF AMERICA

THE MELTING-POT MISTAKE

FOREWORD

It has been widely believed by publicists who write about conditions in the United States that individuals of many nations and races with varying customs and irreconcilable moral codes are issuing from our great metropolises as a type of supermen. The fallacy in this belief has for some time been evident to careful students of our contemporary history, but it took the Great War to open the eyes of an uncritical and indulgent public.

What is the mistake in this notion that New York, Chicago, and other principal American cities are racial and national smelting plants? The idea is largely supported by a mass of unreasoning sentiment, which Mr. Fairchild challenges by plainly stating the observed facts. He shows what social implications are involved in this false symbol of the melting pot and what the essential conditions are of a healthy attitude towards the whole problem of making true citizens out of aliens. This fourth of the books on American nationalism answers, in the light of recent research, those questions that persistently arise regarding the effect of immigration on the vigor and permanence of our life as a nation.

HENRY BASS HALL,
General Editor.

CONTENTS

CHAPTER		PAGE
	Foreword	v
I	Symbols	3
II	The Factor of Race	13
III	The Factor of Nationality	37
IV	Group Contacts	57
V	A Nation in the Making	82
VI	A New Menace	107
VII	The Meaning of Assimilation	136
VIII	Americanization	156
IX	Enforced Patriotism	172
X	The Meaning of America	197
XI	The Making of Americans	221
XII	The Duty of America	247
	Index	263

THE MELTING-POT MISTAKE

CHAPTER I

Symbols

IF "an evil generation seeketh a sign" a mentally harassed and overtaxed generation seeks a symbol. The mind that is wearied with multitudinous demands for judgment upon programs and policies yearns for a simplification of its problems. It wants to have them presented in tabloid form, condensed and visualized in some vivid catch phrase, slogan, or figure of speech. And this is not mere intellectual indolence or torpidity. In the present complicated and headlong organization of society, when the interests of every individual form a network over the globe, and matters of moment rush upon him like telegraph poles along the path of an express train, we are all of us continually called upon to form opinions about a great many more things than we can possibly find time to inform ourselves about by first-hand investigation. This is particularly true in a democratically governed community where not only matters of personal well-being but of national prosperity lay legitimate claim to the attention of the conscientious citizen. A presidential campaign descends upon us, and we discover that in order to vote intelligently and patriotically we must know the truth about Teapot Dome and Elk Hills, about the League of Nations and the tariff — always the tariff — about the Roman Catholic Church and the Ku Klux Klan and their place in American politics, about the Dawes Plan, about surtaxes and excess profits taxes, about bonuses to soldiers and salaries to postal clerks, about government ownership and the minimum wage, about a host of major and minor personalities. This is only a quadrennial climax and condensation of the requirements which every day's experience makes upon our deliberative faculties.

So collectively we devise all sorts of expedients to relieve ourselves individually of the necessity of examination and investigation. In order to free ourselves from the burden of looking personally into the sources of the family meat supply we arrange to have wholesome meat stamped "U. S. Government Inspected." In order to get some assurance, which we could not possibly get for ourselves, as to the quality of the medicines we buy, we pass a national pure drug law and have products labeled accordingly. In buying silverware we simply look for the word "Sterling" and, if we find it, put our minds at ease. A trade-mark is often the most valuable asset of a manufacturing concern.

All this does very well in the realm of material commodities. Here quality is a tangible thing, standards are definite, uniformity is both possible and desirable. We are quite willing to trust the expert, knowing that his knowledge is far superior to our own, that he has access to the facts such as we could never hope to have, and that there is little likelihood that his judgment will be warped by idiosyncrasies of temperament or taste or by personal bias of any kind. But when we enter the realm of ideas the situation changes. The importance of correct judgments increases, while the opportunities for personal investigation and the possibilities of dependable symbolization diminish. We sit through a movie film, "Passed by the Board of Censors", and go away wondering, what if this is good, could the bad be? Wondering, also, how much of the artistic value of the picture has been sacrificed to somebody's ideas of propriety, and how many other films of much greater artistic merit never get their chance on the silver screen at all. Yet we know all too well that there must be some effective selection of the matter displayed before a pleasure-seeking public which can not — if it would — protect itself in advance. "The Beggar's Opera" comes to town and after the first performance the Chief of Police is flooded with complaints from persons who have spent more energy ferreting out every racy allusion in the book than in trying to catch the gay spirit of the rollicking performance. So the Chief details Officer Maloney to attend the next presentation and report whether the show shall be permitted to run or not. And then we wonder whether, after all, a specially designated body, chosen for the presumed technical qualifications of its members, is not a more reliable guarantor of artistic merit and preserver of public morals than this haphazard appraiser.

However, the moral code is a fairly definite thing. There may indeed be a wide debatable middle ground, but the extremes on both sides are easily recognized and generally conceded. Even art has its accepted canons, and there are judges whom the average layman is glad to follow. The great difficulties arise in connection with the problems of political, economic, and social relationships. Here the facts are diffuse, intangible, remote, and, worst of all, are constantly changing. And mere facts, even though we could get them, are not enough. Correct opinions require not only investigation and examination but also thought and reasoning. This imposes a burden quite unbearable by most of us. In a class by itself stands religion; here there are no facts at all in the rigidly scientific sense, but instead, personal experience, faith, intuition, and belief. Here, then, is the maximum need for authoritative labeling and vivid symbolization.

The fact that it is these very political, economic, and social affairs that call for the exercise of our functions as citizens, in the voting booth and elsewhere, makes the difficulty of forming correct independent judgments about them particularly aggravating and particularly dangerous. What hope is there for the progress of a self-governing community if ninety-nine per cent. of the votes cast, of the speeches made, of the editorials penned, of the signatures to petitions, are based on ignorance more or less dense? Yet if we attempt to inform ourselves adequately on even a tithe of the grave problems that press upon a modern society we find ourselves with no time whatever left for the fulfillment of that primary duty of the good citizen, the support of himself and his family. Is it any wonder that we hail the interpreter who can squeeze the essence out of a program or a situation, distil it into a single pulsating drop of meaning, and present it to us to be comprehended and accepted or rejected at a stroke? We all have certain mental classifications or categories — including those which Walter Lippman so illuminatingly discusses as "stereotypes"— in which we have perfect confidence. If some one will only label or epitomize a specific program or policy so that we can summarily fit it into its proper category we will have no difficulty in making up our mind. Let some one we trust merely tell us that a certain measure is "Bolshevistic" and that is enough. We are all ready to jump on the chairs and cheer for the "100 per cent. American" idea. A "conservative" proposition will cleave an audience neatly in two. "Capitalism" and "Socialism" arouse contrasting emotions in the average mind. A "War to make the World safe for Democracy" swings over many a wavering idealist, while the "pacifist" is submerged in the torrential scorn of the herd.

The trouble is, the interpreter may be wrong. He may be wrong in two ways; he may not have all the facts, and he may not draw the same conclusion from the facts that you would. This does not mean that your conclusion would be right. The interpreter's conclusion is wrong for you because it is not your conclusion, and, by the same token, yours would be wrong for him. There is also a chance that you may both be wrong because the category corresponding to the symbol used may be very different in your two minds. "Government paternalism", "un-American", "the expansion of industry", "patriotism" may call up very different images in the mind of the listener from those intended by the speaker.

Democratic processes, to be wholly safe and effective, require that popular decisions should result from the consensus of judgments of the largest possible number and variety of individuals, each forming his conclusions independently on the maximum basis of facts. It is this balancing of individual judgments, rather than any superior mastery of facts, that gives democracy an advantage in stability and soundness over any form of oligarchy. A small, powerful governing clique can very easily acquire a higher average grasp of facts than the common people as a body, but its judgment upon them is bound to be partial. Yet to the extent that any individual in a democratic electorate lacks essential facts his conclusion is quite likely to be erroneous, and the probability of a correct general decision is reduced by just so much.

This brings us back where we started from. We simply can not get all the facts on all the problems. If we are to form independent judgments at all we must of necessity be guided largely by labels and symbols. It is fundamentally important, then, that the interpreters be both honest and acute, and that the symbols be authentic as well as realistic.

These were the facts which gave to Israel Zangwill's little drama, "The Melting-Pot", when it appeared in 1909, a significance quite disproportionate to its literary importance. For one hundred years and more a stream of immigration had been pouring into the United States in constantly increasing volume. At first this movement had attracted little attention, and such feelings as it aroused were mainly those of complacency and satisfaction. As the decades rolled by certain features of the movement created considerable consternation and a demand sprang up for some form of governmental relief. In time this relief was granted, and the popular concern died down. In general, however, during practically the whole of the nineteenth century the attitude of the American people toward immigration was one of easy-going, tolerant indifference when it was not actually welcome. But as the century drew to a close evidences of popular uneasiness and misgiving began to display themselves. These were due in part to changes in the social and economic situation in the United States, in part to changes in the personal and social characteristics of the immigrants, and in part to repeated warnings issued by those whose professional activities and opportunities gave them a wider access to the facts of immigration than was possible to the average citizen. In particular the American people began to ponder about the ultimate effect upon its own vitality and solidarity of this stupendous injection of foreign elements. Could we stand it, and if so, how long? Were not the foundations of our cherished institutions already partially undermined by all these alien ideas, habits, and customs? What kind of a people were we destined to become physically? Was the American nation itself in danger? Immigration became a great public problem, calling for judgment.

Then came the symbol, like a portent in the heavens. America is a Melting-Pot. Into it are being poured representatives of all the world's peoples. Within its magic confines there is being formed something that is not only uniform and homogeneous but also finer than any of the separate ingredients. The nations of the world are being fused into a new and choicer nation, the United States.

The figure was a clever one — picturesque, expressive, familiar, just the sort of thing to catch the popular fancy and lend itself to a thousand uses. It swept over this country and other countries like wild fire. As always, it was welcomed as a substitute for both investigation and thought. It calmed the rising wave of misgiving. Few stopped to ask whether it fitted the phenomena of assimilation. Few inquired whether Mr. Zangwill's familiarity with the intricate facts of immigration were such as to justify him in assuming the heavy responsibility of interpreter. America was a Melting-Pot, the apparent evidences of national disintegration were illusions, and that settled it.

It would be hard to estimate the influence of the symbol of the melting pot in staving off the restriction of immigration. It is certain that in the popular mind it offsets volumes of laboriously compiled statistics and carefully reasoned analyses. It is virtually beyond question that restriction would have come in time in any case. How soon it would have come without the Great War must remain a matter of conjecture. Be that as it may, when the concussions of that conflict had begun to die down the melting pot was discovered to be so badly cracked that it is not likely ever to be dragged into service again. Its day was over. But this did not mean that the real facts of immigration had suddenly become public property. Our symbol had been shattered, but we had not yet, as a people, been able to undertake the extensive investigation necessary to reveal the true nature of the case. The history of post-war movements is replete with evidences of the gross misconceptions of the meaning and processes of assimilation which characterized many even of those who devoted themselves directly to the problem. Even to-day, in spite of the fact that there is perhaps no other great public problem on which the American people is so well educated as on immigration, there is yet great need of a clearer understanding of the tremendous task that still confronts us. We know now that the Melting-Pot did not melt, but we are not entirely sure why. We suspect that that particular figure of speech was an anomaly, but we have not yet found a more appropriate one to take its place. We are a little in doubt as to whether so complicated a phenomenon as assimilation can be adequately represented by any symbol at all. Perhaps there is no short cut to a comprehension of this great problem, and he who would form a sound independent judgment must resign himself to the laborious methods of investigation and thought.

There is a general agreement that in connection with its great immigration movement the United States tried to do something and failed. What was this thing that it tried to do? Why did it fail? Is there still a menace in the results of that failure? Was there ever a possibility of success under the old conditions? Is there hope of escaping the consequences of failure under present conditions? If so, by what means may that hope be realized? These are some of the questions intimately bound up with the fallacy of the Melting-Pot.

CHAPTER II

The Factor of Race

THE central idea of the melting-pot symbol is clearly the idea of unification. That is an idea which needs no logical demonstration to command general acceptance. Every one realizes, almost intuitively, that in any community, particularly a democratic one, unity is one of the essentials of stability, order, and progress. Every American citizen will admit without argument that if immigration threatens the national unity of the United States it is a matter of grave concern. The purpose of the melting-pot figure was to convince the American people that immigration did not threaten its unity, but tended to produce an even finer type of unity. It failed because it did not take account of the true nature of group unity, of the conditions of its preservation, or of the actual consequences of such inroads upon unity as are involved in an immigration movement.

As we survey the world of to-day we are impressed with the fact that group unity is one of the most important factors with which mankind has to reckon. We see the human species divided up into numerous well-defined units, each with certain distinctive characters of its own, each knit together by very powerful ties, each seeking its own interests in preference to, often in opposition to, the interests of others. We call these groups by various names — nations, countries, peoples, races, states, societies. Often one of these names more accurately describes a given group than another. But whatever the name, and whatever the minor distinctions between kinds of groups, the primary fact remains that it is upon the basis of these groups that many vitally important world alignments take place. It is by groups that men trade, develop art and literature, acquire land, seek political aggrandizement, and — most important of all — make war. The world would be an entirely different place to live in if these group demarcations did not exist.

Immigration involves a flow of population between various of these groups. It consequently has an immediate bearing upon group unity, particularly that of the receiving group. In order to understand its significance it is necessary to have in mind the essential facts as to the origin and nature of human groups. As far back as knowledge reaches group organization is found to be characteristic of the human species. In general, as we go back over the course of human evolution we find these groups diminishing in size and eventually in number. The consensus of opinion of scientists is that if we could go back to the very beginning of man's existence we should find a single

THE FACTOR OF RACE

small group, living probably somewhere on the high central plateau of Asia. Among the members of this group there would be virtually complete unity, with only such minute individual variations as distinguish the members of any restricted species of animals.

It appears, then, that the present varieties of the human family have been developed out of an original uniform type.[1] It will help in the understanding of modern group characteristics to trace the processes by which the present diversity was produced. The physical features of this original group of human beings have been quite conclusively determined, and are familiar to almost every one to-day. In general, they resembled much more closely those of a gorilla or chimpanzee than a modern civilized man. The body was covered with a thick coat of brownish hair, the skin of the face where it was exposed was brown and wrinkled, the jaw was heavy and projecting, the eyes deep-set and surmounted by heavy ridges of bone, the nose flat and broad, the forehead low and sloping, the head set well forward on a thick, muscular neck, the arms long and powerful, the legs relatively short and weak, and the posture stooping.

The mental traits of these primitive creatures harmonized with the physical. The level of their intel-

[1] The acceptance of the polygenetic theory of the origin of man, preferred by a few students, does not seriously affect the arguments in the following pages. It simply throws the beginnings of race a stage or two farther back, thereby increasing rather than diminishing the significance of racial demarcations.

ligence was only slightly above that of a modern ape. Their actions were governed by instinct almost as completely as those of an orang-utan. They were dependent for their livelihood upon such supplies as Nature furnished ready to hand. Like every non-human species they were adapted to a certain physical environment, and could not have lived outside of that environment any more than a polar bear could live on Waikiki Beach or a sperm whale in Lake Champlain. In other words, they had a restricted range or habitat, determined by the extent of the particular features of climate, topography, flora, and fauna to which their own organic structure was adjusted.

Nevertheless, in spite of these lowly characteristics, early man must have had some unique and distinctive traits which marked him off as an independent species and destined him to an unparalleled career of world domination. We may never know what all these distinctive qualities were, but we are pretty certain about two of them. One of them was a peculiarly fertile and adaptable brain, capable of development to an unprecedented point. The other was an opposable thumb, that is, a thumb whose tip can be placed squarely against the tips of the fingers, making possible delicate manipulation and a variety of manual processes. This latter trait man probably shared with some of his non-human kinsmen — the higher apes possess it to-day. It alone could never have raised him to his present high estate. But neither could the brain alone. It was the combination of these two traits, supported doubtless by other minor peculiarities, that produced the result.

Thus man started his existence as a new species, with certain distinct advantages, but with a very hard road to travel. He had to make his way in the face of very severe competition. The struggle for existence in Nature was just as keen and bitter then as it is now. The supplies of Nature were limited, and man had to fight for everything he got. His most dangerous rivals were those anthropoid species most closely related to him, and therefore most similar to him in the demands they made upon Nature. The numerical increase of human beings must have been exceedingly slow for many tens of thousands of years. Nevertheless increase took place, just because of the specific advantages with which man was equipped. Eventually this increase reached the point where man's original habitat was filled up.[1] There were as many men living in the area to which man was adapted as Nature supplied subsistence for.

Man thus found himself face to face with one of the great fundamental laws of Nature, the law of stationary population. Every species sooner or later

[1] It is obvious that a deterioration in the supporting power of the land would have the same effect as an increase in the number of the species in producing a crowding of the habitat. This has doubtless occurred in many important instances.

in its evolution finds itself brought up sharply against this law, and every species but man has succumbed to it. When a species has increased up to the point where Nature supplies no more food its increase has stopped, and from that time on its numbers have remained fixed unless some great change in natural conditions has altered the terms of its existence. Man alone, of all the higher animals at least, has been able to escape out of his original habitat and extend his range until it covers practically the entire land surface of the globe. He has done this primarily by means of a progressive adaptation to the requirements of different environments. For some reason, or combination of reasons, man has been able to make the various adaptations necessary to fit him for life in every environment on earth without losing his specific unity. Other types of animals which have spread widely over the earth's surface have undergone such extreme changes that they have broken up into separate species.

In this process of progressive adaptation is to be found the first basis of group differentiation. It is therefore important to understand just why and how this adaptation took place and what is the nature of the results.

It has been observed above that every living species is adapted to some particular environment and also that no two individuals of a given species are exactly identical. This last fact is due to the principle of

THE FACTOR OF RACE

variation which operates throughout all organic beings, and brings it about that no two members, even of the same brood from the same mother, are completely alike. It follows that some individuals are more closely adapted to the surrounding environment than others. As long as the environment remains constant those individuals which are most closely adapted are those that come nearest to the average or type of the species. Those individuals which vary minutely on either side of the average will be able to survive, though with a slight handicap. But those which differ too widely from the type will not be able to hold their own in the fierce struggle for existence and will be eliminated. Thus the typical features of the species are kept constant.

Now at any given time there are always some members of the species living on the very edge of the habitat, that is, in close proximity to a slightly different environment. Among the offspring of these individuals there will be some whose variations constitute a handicap in the regular environment but afford an advantage in the adjacent environment. Some of those with these peculiarities will almost certainly drift over into this new environment and so be able to survive. Of their offspring, those will have the best chance of survival in this new environment which inherit the favorable peculiarities of their parents. Thus this variation tends to be perpetuated. Furthermore, some of these offspring will have variations fitting them to move still farther into the new environment, and here the process will be repeated. Differences in environmental features are the cause of changes in the characteristics of species. Variations occur in all directions according to the law of chance, but only those variations are perpetuated which happen to accord with some slightly different environment into which the individual which possesses them may find his way. If for some reason the original environment undergoes a change the same process, of course, takes place. These developments are indescribably slow, but given sufficient time they will eventually produce a distinctly different type. This new type is at first known as a "variety" of the old species. But as the process goes on the changes at last become so marked that the new type can no longer be considered to belong to the old species: a new species has come into being.

It was undoubtedly by such a method as this that mankind first began to separate into distinct types. We know something of the pathways and directions by which the outposts of the species made their way by infinitesimal stages out of the original central Asian habitat into new environments. Certain well-defined channels led northward and northeastward, into the inhospitable plains of Siberia and eventually across the Bering Sea into the northwest corner of the North American continent and thence southward until the whole of the western hemisphere was

THE FACTOR OF RACE

peopled. Other channels led eastward into the fertile plains of China. Still others took a southwesterly direction and led the primitive pioneers who followed them into Asia Minor, Africa, and thence northward into Europe. In every case the spread of the human species could take place only so fast as the physical variations could be developed necessary for life in each new environment. And in every case it was the contact with a new environment which was responsible for the perpetuation of these variations.

As observed above, man alone of all the higher species has been able to carry this process of variation to the extremities of the earth without losing his specific unity. Instead of having several more or less closely related species of men, as there are species of wolves, or bears, or sparrows, we have one great inclusive human species divided up into a number of varieties. To these varieties we correctly apply the term "the races of man."

The primary basis of group unity is therefore racial.

This being the case, it is essential to understand exactly what the nature of race is, what racial traits are and how they are transmitted, and what bearing race has on the perpetuation of group identity. This is the more necessary because of the extreme vagueness and looseness with which the word is used, and the indefiniteness of the idea it conveys, not only in everyday conversation but even in would-be scientific dissertations.

From the foregoing discussion it is clear that race is something that we share with all organic species. It is strictly and exclusively a biological fact. Whatever influences of race we experience come to us because we are animals. A human race is a group of men more closely related to each other by physiological kinship than they are to the members of other races, because they have more nearly a common ancestry. The ancestral lines of the members of a single race draw together sooner than do those of different races. Of course, as has been shown, the lines of all races eventually draw together into a great common stock. It is obvious, then, that race is a relative term. All men are physiologically related to each other. All men have the same general ancestry, and no two men have an identical ancestry except brothers and sisters. The question of race is a question of degrees of relationship. It is not surprising, therefore, that there should be a wide difference in practice, even among scientific anthropologists, as to the degree of kinship which shall constitute a race. In the first place, we often speak of the entire species as the "human race." We are almost unanimous in referring to the great primary divisions of the species as races — the yellow, brown, black, red, and white races, to take a familiar classification. The next step is to apply the word "race" to subdivisions of one of these primary groups, and this, too, we quite commonly do. For example, it is quite customary now to refer to the European branches of the white race as the "Mediterranean", "Alpine", and "Nordic" races. Not infrequently we go even further than this and speak of the subdivisions of some of these groups as races, — for instance, the "Libyan", "Iberian", "Ligurian", and "Pelasgian" races, components of the Mediterranean race.

No serious confusion need arise from this indefinite use of the word race, provided the crucial fact is kept constantly in mind that racial affiliations are strictly biological. No harm is likely to be done by using the word race to apply to several different gradations in a classification of man, provided the classification itself is based on heredity and kinship. The danger of fallacy lies in applying the term race to groupings which are not based on physical kinship or common ancestry, but on some entirely different principle of group unity.

The primary period of population movement, already described, during which mankind was gradually forcing its way into new environments by a process of slow physical adaptation, may conveniently be designated the "period of race formation." The movement itself may be distinguished from other types of population movement by the term "dispersion." Some of the features which mark it off sharply from all subsequent forms of population movement are its slowness, its essentially instinctive basis, its lack of conscious direction or even perception by those who took part in it, and in particular its lack of a definite destination. Dispersion is characteristically a movement *away* rather than a movement *to*. Its basis is found in the natural urge to escape the law of stationary population, and its direction is determined simply by the conditions of least resistance. One further feature of dispersion, of very great importance to the understanding of modern population problems, is that it was a peaceful movement. This was due to the fact that it was a movement into humanly uninhabited territory. These primitive pioneers were not encroaching on the preserves of any previous settlers. This does not mean, by any means, that the movement was easy or unopposed. There were obstacles in abundance. But they were obstacles set by Nature not by man. Man had to fight his way, but his opponents were creatures on a lower level than himself. There was no conflict of man with man, human group with human group. It was this fact that made the movement possible, for, as one keen student has put it, "Man alone stops man." In the strict sense, therefore, true dispersion lacks the military, hostile, forcible aspects which have characterized so much of later migration. It was a movement which benefited all concerned, those who stayed as well as those who went.

The formation of races resulted from this type of movement, as has already been hinted, in two ways. In the first place, the process of movement broke

THE FACTOR OF RACE

mankind as a whole into separate kin groups. The stream of germ plasm which flowed through the species was divided into a number of independent currents. These remained quite definitely separated from each other, first because they flowed into regions marked off by difficult barriers of mountain, ocean, or jungle, and secondly because the very fact that each group developed an adaptation to a particular environment prevented it, under the primitive conditions that prevailed, from moving over into any other environment. Thus the principles of isolation and segregation kept these streams of germ plasm from mingling with each other and so losing their respective identities. Nor was there any return current back to the original seats. This was due partly to the fact that barriers which will be overcome in the effort to escape starvation will not be attacked for any lesser reasons, and more importantly to the fact that the pressure in the older areas which occasioned the movement in the first instance still exerted itself in the same direction. Thus dispersion formed races primarily because it divided mankind into distinct and isolated kin groups.

The second way by which dispersion caused the formation of races was that it necessitated those physical modifications to which reference has repeatedly been made. In a very sweeping way it may be said that there were developed as many separate races as there were great distinct habitation areas on the earth's surface. Each of these areas demanded its own particular features on the part of the men who were to survive in it. Just what the relationship is between the requirements of a given environment and the traits of the race that found its area of characterization there has not yet been fully explained. In a general way it seems clear that the heavily pigmented skin of the Negro is an advantage in the hot, moist climate of the tropics. It is conceivable that the air pockets formed by his kinky hair may also afford protection from the extreme heat of the sun. Conversely the blue eyes and fair skin of the Nordic appear to have some advantage in the less intense, cold light of the north. Yet the Eskimos, in a somewhat similar environment, have dark hair and eyes. There is little doubt that sexual selection also played its part in determining the result. As distinctive traits began to develop in a given group they would naturally come to be thought of as admirable, beautiful, and right. Thus those individuals who possessed them in the most marked degree would be likely to mate earliest and oftenest, and so these traits would tend to be perpetuated and accentuated. If, for example, we can imagine the time when the Nordic race was just beginning to develop, we can easily conceive that men would tend to choose for their mates the lightest-haired members of the opposite sex, and so would the women, in so far as they had anything to say about it. It seems hardly

THE FACTOR OF RACE 27

probable, however, that natural selection in its strictest sense and sexual selection, working together, were the sole factors in the development of the characteristic features of the different races. There may have been some inherent predisposition latent in these separate streams of germ plasm, as Bergson has suggested in his stimulating discussion of "Creative Evolution."

Whatever the causes, however, the result is manifest. The racial groups which are characterized by community of physical kinship are also identified by distinct physical features. These are what we ordinarily speak of as "race traits" or "characters", and it is needful to have in mind clearly just what they are and how they operate.

It should be clear by now that all true racial traits are exclusively hereditary. They are carried on from generation to generation by means of "genes" or "determiners" in the germ plasm of each race. Their appearance in the body of any individual is due to the fact that he has the corresponding genes in his germ plasm, and not to any other cause. No racial trait can ever be acquired, nor can it ever be lost by an individual as a result of the experiences of his lifetime. What we are racially, we are from the moment not only of birth, but of conception, and such we remain until we die. It follows that the individual is not in the slightest degree responsible for his racial affiliations or his racial traits. He was not consulted in advance as to what racial traits he would prefer and he has no power to alter or dispose of a single one of them. Moreover, he has no control whatever over the racial traits which he will pass on to his offspring. If any individual is dissatisfied with the racial traits with which he is endowed, his only recourse for himself is artificially to conceal them or inhibit their display in his own person so far as that is possible, and his only hope for his offspring is to mate with a person of a different race, in which case his children get a mixture of racial traits, his own contribution being exactly what it would have been if he had mated with one of his own race. Fortunately, as will appear later, most individuals, at least in an unsophisticated state, are quite content with their racial affiliations and would not change them if they could.

The use of the words "racial traits" and "characters" in the plural suggests the fact that one's racial make-up is a composite of a number of distinct units. This harmonizes with the modern theory of inheritance, which holds that one's entire heredity is composed of separate units — what the biologists call "unit characters"— which are transmitted from generation to generation independently of each other, and never fuse or coalesce, each having its own determiner or gene in the germ plasm. From the point of view of racial interpretation, accordingly, the inherited traits of each individual are composed of two

THE FACTOR OF RACE

groups. The first group includes all those traits which he as a human being shares with all other human beings, the common features of the species. The second group includes those traits which he shares only with the other members of his racial group, the distinctive features of the race. The narrower the definition of race, obviously, the smaller does this second group become. The first group, however, is vastly larger than the second group even on the most inclusive interpretation of race. Men as a whole are much more alike than they are different. The general structure, all the important organs and members, all the basic life processes are essentially similar if not virtually identical in all the members of all the races.

It is probably much more than a coincidence that most of the important features in which there are characteristic differences between races are associated with the head. It is in the head that the differentiation of the human species from other animal species has been particularly developed, and it is logical that it should be in the head that the specialization of the biological divisions of the human species should be carried to the highest point. The outstanding exception to this rule is found in skin color, which is so very marked as to be adopted as the commonest basis of primary racial classification. This is the feature which most immediately and most forcefully impresses the layman, in whose consciousness it probably holds a larger place than any other single race criterion. Other racial traits not connected with the head are the relative proportions of the arms and legs, and other portions of the body, the distribution of fat over the frame, stature, and the shape of the foot. There are also certain differences in susceptibility to, and immunity from, certain diseases, which may eventually be found to depend upon actual differences in the constitution of the blood.

Of the distinctive features of the head, some are found in the fleshy covering of the skull, some in the brain matter contained within the skull, and some in the skull itself. Each of these classes has its particular importance in certain connections. For the scientific purposes of the anthropologist the features of the skull are of paramount importance, partly because the skull is the only part of the head which is ordinarily preserved for any considerable time after death, and so makes possible comparisons between modern and ancient men, and partly because the features of the skull lend themselves peculiarly well to representation by indices, thus facilitating minute and exact measurements and comparisons. Of the various indices in use, probably the most important is what is known as the "cranial" or "cephalic index", which is the proportion (expressed in percentage) between the greatest breadth and the greatest length of the skull looked at from above. Others are the proportion between the greatest breadth

THE FACTOR OF RACE 31

and the greatest height, looked at from in front, and the proportion between length and height. Indices of the eye socket and the nasal opening are also regarded as of much significance. A further measurement of the skull which, while not in the form of an index, nevertheless allows of exact comparisons, is what is known as the "facial angle." This, simply described, represents the slope of the face from the upper jaw to the forehead, and is expressed in degrees. The increasing size of this angle indicates the progression from the low brow to the high brow. Other features of the skull of much importance are the bony ridges above the eye sockets, the cheek bones, the cranial sutures, various ridges on the surface of the skull, and the point at which the spinal column joins the skull.

It is clear that all of these features have very little direct practical bearing upon the attitudes and relationships of the members of different races toward one another, for the simple reason that they are not perceptible by the ordinary processes of observation. If all racial differences were of this type, the average man would seldom be aware that he was dealing with a person of another race. From the point of view of ordinary personal contacts, the most significant features of the head are those on the surface, including such matters as the form and color of the hair, the color and shape of the eyes, the shape of the nose and lips, and the general contour and aspect of the face. It is almost exclusively by these tests, coupled with skin color, that most of us ordinarily form our judgments as to the race of other individuals.

The distinctive features of the brain are among the most elusive of all race traits; they are certainly the most important from the point of view of social relationships. Upon these organic differences depend any intellectual, emotional, or psychical traits of any kind that can accurately be regarded as racial. For only physical brain matter and nerve connections are inherited, and only that which is inherited is racial. Just what the truly racial features of intellect, disposition, temperament, and emotion may be is still almost wholly *terra incognita*. It is a temptation, to which all too many writers and speakers yield, to talk glibly of the psychical qualities of various human groups as if their physical basis and racial character had been scientifically determined. In fact, there is a great field of knowledge here which is only just beginning to be explored. Our conclusions as to the kinds and degrees of psychical specialization which are genuinely racial must be held in suspense until research has been carried much further. But whatever the results of this research may be as to details, there seems to be little room for doubt that these psychical contrasts play a much more important part in impeding harmonious action between groups than the external or narrowly physical aspects. Just as we, individually, choose our friends more for their spiritual traits than for their physical, so the relations between groups of men depend much more on their respective reactions to ideas and other psychical stimuli than upon the physical appearance or the anthropological classification of their members. We can quickly get used to novel or even unattractive outward appearances, but we can never quite adjust ourselves to those whose fundamental spiritual processes have nothing in common with our own.

Apparently the process of race formation stopped long ago. As far as available evidence goes, it seems that the racial differentiation of mankind at the beginning of the historical period was virtually identical with what it is now. Paintings on the walls of Egyptian tombs four thousand years old show racial types which can easily be identified with those now inhabiting that region. Lothrop Stoddard tells of examining a set of little clay figures found in Egypt and dating from about the year 600 B.C. which reveal the same features, though in this case there are some racial types which can not be assigned to any living races now known. The principal changes that have taken place within the historical period have been in the nature of the mixing of races. These are of the greatest importance, to be sure, and call for some detailed consideration.

The period of dispersion and race formation occupied unquestionably much the longer portion of man's career on earth. Its processes were infinitesimally slow, and its scope covered the entire habitable globe.[1] But it could not go on forever. Its end was brought about chiefly by two great alterations in the situation. The first was the eventual exhaustion of the uninhabited regions of the world. The time came at last when there were no more unoccupied lands for the surplus members of humanity to move into. Every habitation area on earth had its own particular group, and each environmental district had done its work in developing an adapted type of man. The second factor in the end of the period of race formation was the development of a distinctly human culture or civilization on the part of the human animal. This introduced a new epoch into human affairs in two ways. First, it reduced and eventually eliminated the necessity of physical adaptation as a condition of movement into diverse environments by substituting for it the possibility of artificial adaptation. Modern civilized man can move freely all over the globe, and live fairly normally in any part of it. It is true that there are some limitations which he has not been able to escape. The white man apparently takes a risk when he attempts to get in immediate contact with the soil of the tropics, and white

---

[1] It should be observed that the period of dispersion is a stage in social evolution, not a chronological epoch. Its end can not be identified, even approximately, with any fixed date. It came at very different times in different sections of the earth's surface, earliest in the areas of earliest human settlement, latest in the most recently populated regions. Dispersion was still going on along the fringes of human expansion long after more conscious — and quite different — forms of movement had developed in the older areas.

women are gravely handicapped in carrying out their part of the reproduction of the species in these regions. But, broadly speaking, the development of civilized arts of life has made possible very radical changes in environment without physical adaptation.

The second way in which civilization has affected racial factors is by providing the means of rapid movement from one region to another. These means include both the material or mechanical conveyances themselves, and the knowledge and other psychical factors which are requisite for the movement of people either individually or in masses.

If the pressure of population had ceased to operate with the end of the period of race formation the whole subsequent experience of mankind would have been entirely different. But, as we know all too well, it did not cease. The impulse was at least as strong as before for each group to dispose of its surplus members by crowding them out into new areas. But now there were no unoccupied lands for them to appropriate. If they moved at all they had to move into the territory of some other group. There thus emerged a new era which may be called the "period of race contact", and, unfortunately, also "race conflict." The inevitable result of race contact, even on fundamentally hostile terms, is race mixture. As some one has said, the relations between racial groups struggling for possession of the same land are likely to be alternately martial and marital. While the period of race mixture has been very much shorter in time than the period of race formation, its processes have been decidedly more rapid. Consequently, there has been a vast amount of race mixture accomplished, particularly in those areas which are by nature favorable to the movements of peoples. As a rule, the racial purity of groups is in inverse ratio to the accessibility of the regions they inhabit. The pure races of to-day are to be found in the remote, isolated corners of the earth.

As may be easily understood, however, there can be racial identity and racial distinction without racial purity. If only two races are mixed, the resulting type may be almost as distinct and definite as a pure race. As a matter of fact, in spite of the long centuries of race mixture, it still remains true that in most of the great habitation areas of the globe the natives are characterized at least by a typical racial preponderance if nothing more. There is still ample racial unity in the leading human groups to make racial traits and racial affiliations fundamental factors in intergroup relationships.

CHAPTER III

THE FACTOR OF NATIONALITY

WHILE the long process of race formation was going on a related, but entirely distinct, development was taking place. Frequent mention has been made in the foregoing pages of the development of a unique human trait, civilization, as a factor in group formation. This factor has played a varied rôle in keeping with its profound importance. Our immediate interest is to examine how it has undergone a process of specialization in many ways analogous to the biological specialization which produced races, with a resultant basis of group unity fully equal in significance to race itself.

The primary purpose of man's civilization is to help him in solving his great life problems. These problems consist mainly in finding means to gratify his various desires, to realize his manifold interests. In accordance with the fact noted above that all men are fundamentally alike, the basic desires and interests of all men are essentially uniform. All men have the same elemental equipment of instincts and appetites, and even the more distinctly human desires and interests are largely similar. All men desire food and shelter, light and warmth; all seek to gratify their impulses to play, to know, to mate;

all long for self-expression and recognition; all desire to have a good opinion of themselves which depends largely on the assurance that they enjoy the good opinion of their fellows.

Some of these desires are primarily individual in their origin and application; others are distinctly social. Practically all of them develop social implications increasing steadily as man moves upward on the evolutionary scale. Accordingly, the various human groups that resulted from the processes of race formation were all occupied with the pursuit of the same great life interests. But the methods developed for the achievement of the dominant social aims were like the sands of the sea for number. No two groups worked out their life problems in the same way. Every group had to have some means of communication as a primary condition of group life. But no two groups developed the same language independently, and even where they started with a similar linguistic basis they very soon drifted apart as soon as group diversity was established. It is estimated that among the half million odd Indians of North America there were "at least sixty-five of the separate stock languages . . . which appear so radically separated from each other that it is believed impossible that they ever should have sprung from the same parent" unless it be at a very remote period.[1] It is interesting to speculate how long the

---

[1] Frederick S. Dellenbaugh, "The North Americans of Yesterday", page 20.

THE FACTOR OF NATIONALITY

English language would remain mutually comprehensible to Englishmen and Americans if an impassable barrier should be set up between those two peoples. For the processes of groups specialization in this respect are still going on. Every group has to have an economic organization to help it in winning its subsistence from the soil. But no two groups have developed the same system. Tools and other instruments and implements have been among the most characteristic of group specialties from the dawn of civilization down to the present. Every social group feels the necessity of some basis of interpreting the relationships between human beings and the unseen powers. But the name of the world pantheon is Legion. So it goes through an almost interminable list — the family institution, dress, food, ornamentation, recreation, the political system, the moral code. In all of these interests group diversities are developed far more numerous and striking than the racial traits themselves.

It would be even more difficult to explain just why a particular solution of a given problem was hit upon by a given group than to explain the origin of race traits. Fortunately, for the present purpose it is quite unnecessary. It is the existence of these groups specializations, not their origin, that is significant. One thing, however, is certain, that for the development of these peculiarities the same factors of isolation and segregation were necessary that were involved in race formation. It therefore followed that in the beginning the development of these two kinds of specialization went along the same lines, and followed exactly the same group demarcations.

There thus arose a very natural confusion which has persisted down to the present moment, not only in the mind of the average layman but also in the mental processes of many who undertake to act as interpreters of these great problems. This is the confusion between race, and this other fundamental basis of group unity. An indication of this confusion is furnished by the fact that there does not exist even a word to definitely indicate the latter. Of all the available terms, that which comes nearest to the idea is "nationality", and rather than follow the academician's expedient of coining a new term out of his inner consciousness it will be well to take this word, give it a restricted meaning, and use it in as scientific a sense as possible. It may be said, therefore, that *the second great basis of group unity is national.*

As long as human groups remained effectually separated from each other the distinction between race and nationality was of neither academic nor practical importance. The two, as has been said, developed simultaneously and coincidently. Each group which was working out its own peculiar scheme of life was originally a racial group. Consequently a

THE FACTOR OF NATIONALITY 41

given group was identifiable by either its racial or its national characteristics. The two being practically indistinguishable naturally appeared to be synonymous or identical. Inasmuch as a certain widely penetrating group of roundheaded individuals had the invariable habit of burying their dead in round barrows it was easy to think of the burial customs as being the same sort of a group trait as the head form. Perhaps the most notable — or notorious — instances of this confusion are to be found in the use of the words "Aryan" and "Celtic" as racial designations. In their correct sense both of these terms apply strictly to national characteristics, and to speak of the Aryan race or the Celtic race is, as one writer has said, just as absurd as to talk about a brachycephalic dictionary or a brunette grammar.

As soon as the era of race mingling set in, however, the distinction between race and nationality became of vital practical importance, because the two exhibit entirely different types of behavior in cases of group contact. And as soon as the age of intelligent social engineering dawned the importance became academic as well as practical, because no constructive social policy can possibly be worked out to govern intergroup relationships which does not take strict account of the difference between these two foundations of unity. One of the chief sources of fallacy in the figure of the melting pot lay in the failure to make this crucial distinction. It will be well, therefore, to examine in somewhat greater detail the nature of national traits and the method of their transmission.

As has been shown, race traits are due solely to inheritance. Race traits are group traits only because community of kinship has been harmonious with the processes of group formation and group maintenance. They are by no means inseparable from group affiliation. An individual takes his race with him wherever he goes and passes it on to his offspring wherever he may be. Two parents of a given race will produce a child of the same race no matter in what sort of a group they may be living at the time of the child's birth. And the child must keep that race until the day of his death no matter into what groups the vicissitudes of life may lead him.

The traits of nationality, on the other hand, are distinctly group realities. They arise solely out of the group relationship. They impress themselves on the individual, but by no means ineradicably. Race is inherited, nationality is acquired. Or, it may be said that race is biologically transmitted, and nationality is socially transmitted. For nationality is passed on from generation to generation just as truly as race, but in an entirely different way. The processes of social transmission are the processes of individual acquirement. As far as the individual is concerned, nationality is an acquired character-

THE FACTOR OF NATIONALITY 43

istic, and must follow the laws of acquired characteristics rather than of inherited traits.

Every individual is born with no nationality at all. He has no language, no dress, no moral code, no religion, no single one of the manifold accomplishments that compose human culture. He is just a little uncivilized animal, with the whole course of cultural evolution to go through with in the years that lie before him, just as in the prenatal period he went through the whole course of biological evolution from the single cell up. The great biogenetic law of recapitulation — "ontogeny repeats phylogeny", the development of the individual is a condensed repetition of the evolution of the species — holds good for the cultural development of the human individual after birth just as for his physical development before birth. But the cultural development is determined by the cultural medium, or mediums, in which his postnatal life is spent, while his physical development is determined by the kind of germ plasm that went into that original embryonic cell.

No national trait is inherited or is present at birth, though there may be some inherited aptitudes that correspond in a general way to certain types of nationality. Thus there is some evidence of slight physical differences in the organs of speech that prevent the members of certain races from completely mastering certain languages. It is also claimed (on rather inadequate grounds), that the Nordic race has a special aptitude for free institutions. There are probably certain inherent variations of temperament, disposition, or even intelligence which facilitate the development by certain racial groups of certain types of institutions.[1] But all of these influences, whatsoever they may actually be, are of the most general sort, and there is the scantiest possible evidence of any inherited tendency to develop a specific national trait. Certainly there is a minimum of ground for believing that long habitude to certain national customs will affect the germ plasm in such a way as to alter any of the physical dispositions. It is related that a certain noted Englishwoman, on a recent visit to the United States, expressed a lively admiration, mingled with surprise, for the beautiful figures of American girls. "After centuries of shaping bodies into the lines of an hour-glass she said it amazed her that such figures survive." She need not have been amazed. Tight lacing is a national characteristic. Waist lines are racial.

There is accordingly no necessary connection between the nationality of parents and that of their children. The only reason why the two are ordinarily the same is that in the usual course of affairs children and parents live in the same social environment. The only sense in which children get their nationality from their parents is that the parents represent the environment to them in a peculiarly

[1] See MacDougall, "The Indestructible Union", pp. 9, 88, 138.

THE FACTOR OF NATIONALITY 45

intimate and potent way. This is a steadily diminishing influence from the time of infancy — when the parents constitute the major part, if not virtually the whole, of the social environment of the child — to full maturity when the parental bond is reduced to a more or less negligible factor, according to the customs of the nationality itself. But let a child be removed from its parents immediately after birth and placed in the midst of a different nationality and it will inevitably acquire the full nationality of the group in which it is brought up. Take a new-born child of Scandinavian parents and place it in a native negro home in the jungles of Africa. At maturity it will have the blond hair, blue eyes, and fair skin (tanned, of course) of its Nordic ancestry, but its language, religion, moral code, habits of life, and whole outlook on the universe will be that of the primitive group of which its foster parents have been a part.

Since the national equipment of an individual consists of traits acquired from the social environment during his lifetime, it follows that it is subject to change as long as life lasts. But the acquisition of national traits takes place much more rapidly and easily during the impressionable, plastic years of infancy and early childhood than in the later periods of life. In general, the receptivity to national impressions diminishes steadily with increasing age. It is really astounding, when one stops to think of it, how much of the important business of life a child has learned by the time it reaches the end of its second year. Yet one never entirely ceases responding to the influence of his environment while he lives. There is always more of nationality than any one individual can fully absorb, and since, as will appear later, nationality is always a more or less dynamic factor, the traits of the individual are constantly called upon to respond to a varying environment. In the case of the ordinary individual who spends virtually his whole life in the midst of a single group environment the process is a harmonious and largely unconscious one. It is when a sudden change in environment takes place, as will be seen, that strain arises.

The channels through which the national group impresses its characteristics upon its individual members include practically every variety of human relationship. As has been observed, the earliest of these, and probably in the long run the most influential, is the family. One after another the church, the school, the playground, the recreation center, the lodge, the shop, the factory, the theater, the political rally, the union, all manner of associations and organizations bring the influence of group standards to bear upon the individual. Some of these institutions owe their existence in part to the necessity of group control over the social unit. Other institutions, the State *par excellence*, have been evolved

THE FACTOR OF NATIONALITY 47

by society directly for the purpose of securing conformity to group requirements. The development of national traits on the part of the individual through participation in these various relationships is neither voluntary nor conscious under ordinary conditions. But it is irresistible. One cannot possibly avoid receiving the imprint of his environment, nor can he modify it even in slight degree until he reaches the age of discrimination and reasoning, and by that time the basic traits of nationality are so deeply graven on his character that there is little scope left for the play of analysis and reason.

In fact, the whole development of nationality has very little direct connection with the reasoning faculty of the human animal. This is possibly one explanation of the tremendous hold it has upon all of us. For the less a given custom or belief is amenable to the processes of logic, the more tenaciously and aggressively do we cling to it as a rule. If a certain doctrine is of such a character that its validity is capable of rational proof or disproof, there is some chance that a man may be led to change his stand upon it. But if it rests solely upon belief, tradition, custom, or habit, no amount of argument can affect it in the least — it is invulnerable to argument. And a very large part of nationality is based almost exclusively upon tradition and wont; that is, upon the uncritical and uncriticized past. It's the way of my fathers and it's good enough for me!

But whatever the explanation, the fact is indubitable that nationality has tremendous inertia and authority, and exercises a prodigious sway over its adherents. The rightness of nationality is absolute, all the more so for the very reason that it seldom occurs to the average individual even to call it in question. Obviously, and necessarily, the rightness of any given nationality is limited to its own adherents. A thousand contradictory nationalities all have an equal degree of rightness. Hence the resounding clash when they are brought into conflict. My language is the finest language in the world. My religion is the only true faith; all other kinds of worshippers are unbelievers, heretics, heathen, gentiles. The way I and my fellows dress is beautiful, decent, sensible — at least, it is the right way. The women of Turkey, as soon as their hair begins to turn gray, dye it a bright red with henna. The finger nails are similarly treated. To an American this seems a ridiculous and unsightly practice. Yet the women of America, even before their cheeks become sallow and wrinkled, dye them a bright red with something or other; their lips receive a similar treatment. And we think this is beautiful. The Turkish man in his moments of leisure (which are numerous) toys ceaselessly with a string of beads. The American man laughs at this childish practice as he strikes his sixteenth match to light his "overdraft" pipe. Chinese girl babies, while they are still too young to have anything to say about it, have their feet tightly bound to increase their beauty, and the "civilized" nations send over missionaries to stop these barbarous practices. And, as like as not, the charming young Westerner who takes up the collection at the women's foreign mission circle totters down the aisle in highheeled pointed shoes that not only deform her feet but throw her whole skeleton out of plumb. We Americans can hardly bear even to look at the pictures of the Botocudos with their horrible plugs of wood inserted in their pendulous lower lips, but we are captivated by a pair of jade earrings sweeping a pair of white shoulders. The Bantu belle in Africa files her teeth into fantastic patterns in order to be "right"; the American belle, in certain walks of life, quite unnecessarily fills her teeth with gold — after all, it's only a question of a letter — while in other circles she prefers to operate on her eyebrows. The young Greek dandy would no more think of shaving off his moustache than the American dandy would think of shaving a tonsure on the crown of his head.

It is easy thus to assume a sophisticated and detached air and poke fun at the traits of one's own nationality as well as at those of others. But satire does not alter the facts, even for the satirist. And when it comes to some of the more fundamental aspects of nationality one finds difficulty in seeing any humor in the situation at all. Matters of the moral code, of standards of decency, of the relations between the sexes before and after marriage, of political institutions, of economic systems, of religion, do not lend themselves to flippant comparisons. And even with respect to the trivial mandates of nationality, though we may laugh at them we nevertheless obey them. Because one has brought himself to believe that the easy flowing garb of some Balkan peasant village is more sensible than a stiff shirt and collar and a swallow-tail coat he does not thereupon wear it to a formal dinner in a metropolitan hotel. As suggested above, both those aspects of nationality which are susceptible to the processes of reason and those which are not become so firmly fixed in the psychic equipment of the individual long before the age of rational analysis is reached that their authority is virtually impregnable.

Nationality, then, is to be thought of as a great spiritual reality, existing much less in the realm of the intellect than in the sentiments and emotions. A certain amount of knowledge is inherent in nationality, but its real essence consists not in what one knows but in how one feels. Nationality is a composite body of ideas and ideals, beliefs, traditions, customs, habits, standards, and morals infused with loyalty, devotion, allegiance, and affection. A group of people who possess and are possessed by such a concrete mass of spiritual values embody that nationality, or, in a slightly different use of the word, constitute a nationality, or *are* a nationality.

THE FACTOR OF NATIONALITY 51

True nationality is something that has been developed only by the human species. The classifications of race apply to the lower organic types very much as they apply to man. The races of man are analogous to the "varieties" of other species. But no other species has developed group demarcations based on differences in its way of life. Nationality is a unique human attribute.

It is natural, therefore, that as man has moved upward along his distinctly human pathway the influence of race upon his activities has steadily decreased in relative importance while that of nationality has correspondingly increased. As has been shown, man's subjection to purely biological factors was eventually reduced to such inferior proportions that the process of actual race differentiation came to an end, though of course the definite race characteristics, already permanently established, have continued to play their very important rôle. While for thousands of years there has been apparently no tendency toward further race specialization, neither has there been any evidence of a tendency for races to lose their characteristic features and converge toward a common type, except through the process of mixture.[1] But nationality has grown steadily

[1] This statement is based upon the assumption that the perpetuation and intensification of the physical variations that distinguish the various races have been caused by the necessity of adaptation to different environments. Modern man, having freed himself from the necessity of physical adaptation even in new environments by the development of artificial adaptation, does not undergo the rigid weeding-out process by which the traits specially appropriate to a given

more complex, more specialized, and more determinative of human destiny. Unless the time comes when all civilization becomes absolutely static, nationality will go on developing as long as man is man. Even though it may be conceived that eventually all mankind will be merged in one great nationality, it will nevertheless be a growing and changing nationality. Nationality is a product of the human mind reflecting itself in group relations. So as long as the human mind continues to develop, and as long as the principle of change remains inherent in group relationships, nationality must continue to be a dynamic factor.

It will be well, perhaps, to attempt to set up a clear distinction between the concepts of "nationality" and "nation." There is by no means a general agreement as to exactly what this distinction is. But possibly the best definition of a nation is a nationality that has achieved an independent political existence. We have become so familiar with the terms "submerged nationalities" and "national minorities" that there is no longer much danger of assuming that the terms "country" or "state" are synonymous with nationality or that every political unit is coterminous with a nationality. The bonds of nationality may run quite independently of those

environment are perpetuated. If it be true that the environment acts in some other way than by natural selection to impress hereditable traits upon the men who feel its influence, then race developments may still take place from mere residence in a certain region. This, however, seems exceedingly doubtful.

THE FACTOR OF NATIONALITY 53

of government. Thus before the War the Polish nationality was partitioned out between three political units, Germany, Austria-Hungary, and Russia, while on the other hand Austria-Hungary, a single political unit, contained several more or less discordant nationalities. Even in some of the new States created out of the débris of the War time has revealed a discouraging lack of that national unity which those who charted the new political boundaries assumed as their guide. In both Czecho-Slovakia and the Kingdom of the Serbs, Croats, and Slovenes (the title itself is ominous) the basis of harmony is very shaky. In the words of one of the most enlightening students of this problem, nationality has been described as "the principle by which individuals who recognize sufficiently strong similarities among themselves aspire to become an independent political community on a common territory."[1] These recognized similarities and this ardent aspiration may exist, and do exist, quite regardless of the political alignments which have resulted from the complicated action of historical forces. A true nation arises when such a group as has been described realizes its aspiration, that is, when a nationality achieves the political control of the geographical area upon which it dwells.

The essence of national coherence is a sufficient

[1] Theodore Ruyssen, "What is a Nationality?" *International Conciliation*, Number 112, page 4. Translated by John Mez.

degree of recognized likeness and community of interest in the great activities of group life to inspire a yearning for "togetherness." In the words of Professor Ross, it is a manifestation of the "we-feeling" as contrasted with the "you-feeling." It is clear that this feeling may vary in intensity, and that accordingly the sense of nationality, and nationality itself, may be weak or strong. As a rule, the larger the number of sentiments and emotions that are shared, and the higher the degree of community of interests, the stronger will be the nationality. But it is by no means necessary that there should be complete similarity and community in all particulars. On the contrary, too great an identity in minor matters, while it adds strength in the sense of intensity to nationality, may, like too much inbreeding, produce flabbiness, lack of stamina, and incapacity for progress. But when there are vital disagreements on fundamental points, when there are serious barriers to like-mindedness, then nationality is weakened. Professor William Graham Sumner used to tell his students at Yale that the United States had no claim to the name of nation because of the presence of so large a negro population, the implication being that between the white and colored races there exist such lively recognitions of dissimilarity that they can never establish the degree of common feeling necessary to true nationality. Different nationalities owe their existence and strength to different com-

THE FACTOR OF NATIONALITY 55

binations or phases of community; there can be no general recipe for national unity.

The question is often raised whether community in religion is an indispensable element in nationality. Let Mr. Ruyssen speak once more:

"A nation once established can dispense with religious unity, whenever the consciousness of national solidarity is strong enough to allow the individual conscience to free itself from any creed, or to worship in private the God within, or to adore the 'Father of all mankind.'"[1]

There could hardly be a better answer. However potent religion is in binding groups together, it is not an absolute requisite for national unity, provided enough other grounds of community exist. In fact, the truth probably is that no single trait is absolutely indispensable to national unity. Even language, as Switzerland, with its common use of German, French, and Italian has so conclusively proved, may be diversified as far as the mass of the common people is concerned, though it is probably necessary that there should be a small intelligent and educated group representing all parts of the country among whom free communication is possible. But when a nationality, for whatsoever reason, has only a few well-established common traits, it is essential that these should be of a fundamental character, including at least two or three out of the

[1] *Op. cit.,* page 20.

following list: language, religion, political ideas, basic moral code, family institution, class feelings. As pointed out later, racial homogeneity, while not a part of nationality, is a powerful bulwark of national feeling. There is reason to believe that it was solely the combination of a common language with a common religion which kept the Greek nationality alive during the long centuries of Turkish domination, and in the end enabled it to achieve its great ambition and become a real nation once more.

Race and nationality, then, are the two universal foundations of group unity. Upon their character and the relations between them depend the great problems which, for a time, we the American people were ready to dismiss from our minds by a light-hearted appeal to the figure of the melting pot.

CHAPTER IV

GROUP CONTACTS

THE primary human groups were characterized by two great types of likeness, — physical similarity or race unity, and cultural similarity or national unity. It is apparently a general law of nature that creatures which are similar to each other are drawn or attracted to each other and find pleasure in companionship and some degree of common action. Thus John Burroughs observes, "Attraction, affiliation, assimilation — like to like, is the rule of life." [1] This same principle is recognized by Professor Giddings when he makes "consciousness of kind" the pivotal point in his whole system of sociology. Accordingly it was natural that among the members of each of these original human groups there should grow up a feeling of sympathy, elementary and limited enough at first, but nevertheless an entirely different kind of emotion from that which was felt toward the members of another group. In fact, the attitude toward the out-group was exactly the reverse; not sympathy — a feeling with — but antipathy — a feeling against. This feeling might vary in intensity from mere dislike or repulsion to active

[1] John Burroughs, "Is Nature Beneficent?" *Yale Review*, 9 : 374.

opposition. In general, the primitive attitude toward outsiders is one of animosity and distrust often reaching extremes of hostility. "He's a stranger, kill him" quite accurately represents the sentiment widely characteristic of tribes which have only partly emerged from the early conditions of isolation. In more recent times this becomes toned down to "He's a foreigner, heave a brick at him", but much of the primal sentiment lingers on in the masses of the most civilized peoples. There was a mediæval law in England which prescribed that if a foreigner was found more than a few yards away from a public highway and did not shout or blow a horn he was to be adjudged a spy and killed at sight. The story is familiar of the more modern Englishman who, after listening to some of the customary complaints fróm a friend who had just returned from a trip to the Continent, terminated the conversation with the remark, "I always told you abroad was a nasty place." John Drinkwater gives a very pertinent illustration of this principle in his delightful sketch of "Rufus Clay the Foreigner", who had moved into a Cotswold neighborhood from a village seventeen miles away and had lived there "'not above ten or twelve years.'" "I discovered that nothing short of two generations of unbroken tenure constitutes native rights. Settlers, if only from the next parish, are foreigners, and openly called so. For casual pass-the-time-of-day acquaintance, even for neighborly talk, this is no particular disability, but if you come with the intention of carrying on business, you are likely to be disillusioned, as Rufus Clay learnt."[1]

Sympathy toward the in-group and antipathy toward the out-group may be regarded as universal human traits. The in-group feeling manifests itself in a multitude of ways, and sometimes reaches amazing extremes. It is not unknown among primitive tribes for the name of the tribe to be synonymous with the word for men. A traveler asking for the name of the tribe will be told, "We are The Men." All other tribes are something less than men. This feeling is a compound of familiarity, pride, self-interest, habit, affection, and loyalty. At its worst, it expresses itself as an overweening ethnic egotism and selfishness. At its best, it appears as exalted patriotic devotion. The champions of German Kultur probably sincerely believed that the world would be the gainer by the extension, even at the point of the bayonet, of this particular brand of national unity. The feeling toward the out-group includes among its components dislike, disgust, misunderstanding, hatred, fear, and various degrees of hostility. Among primitive groups such altruism as exists is confined virtually to the in-group. There is no such thing as an interest in the welfare of mankind in general.

[1] John Drinkwater, "Cotswold Characters", *Yale Review*, 10: 840.

Such were some of the obstacles which had to be faced, the factors which complicated the situation, when the gradual filling up of the earth and the increasing intelligence and mobility of human beings began to promote intergroup relations. By this time men had become fully habituated to acting in groups and responding to the stimulus of group interests. In fact, the sense of group affiliation was often more intense than among more civilized men. This is excellently illustrated in the case of the invasions of the Goths and Vandals, and the other bodies of Teutonic barbarians which swept down into southern Europe in the early centuries of the Christian era. Among these groups the individual could hardly conceive of life apart from his tribe. The tribe was his home, his country, his fatherland. Under such conditions mass movements on the part of the tribe as a whole were almost automatic. So these tribes are found clinging together in distinct units through long centuries of wandering, battle, and various other vicissitudes.

Not only have group sympathy and group antipathy been universal factors in human experience, it is conceivable that they may have had a definite utility in promoting the growth of civilization in its early stages. In an intergroup struggle, that group will succeed, other things being equal, which has the most highly developed sense of common interests, the most efficient community of action, and the most loyal devotion on the part of its members. In other words, in the competition of life between groups, altruism, patriotism, and social efficiency have survival value, and since these factors have been essential to the development of civilization the motive which underlies them, group sympathy, may be considered as having had a distinct usefulness.

It has been remarked that under conditions of virtual segregation the distinction between race and nationality is of no practical significance. So it is only as groups begin to mingle with each other that it becomes necessary to consider the twofold basis of group feeling. As long as a tribe remains by itself it makes little difference whether its community feeling rests upon likeness of physical features or upon likeness in cultural traits, or to what extent it may be distributed between the two. But when groups begin to wander about, to encroach upon each other's territory, to mix their blood, and to copy each other's ways of doing things, it makes all the difference in the world whether sympathy and antipathy will follow the racial factor or the national factor. For while these two factors developed coincidently, they are by no means inseparably bound together. On the contrary, in the course of intergroup contacts, they are very likely to split apart and go off on independent pathways. This is a matter of primary importance and demands some detailed consideration.

At the risk of tedious repetition, let it be stated once more that true racial forces and factors follow the lines of biological continuity exclusively. The only way in which the racial character of a group can be changed is by the introduction of diverse streams of germ plasm carried in the actual physical bodies of persons of a different race. Under such conditions, the change in race that takes place is in the first instance mathematically proportioned to the relative amount of foreign germ plasm represented in the matings that occur within the group. If there is a differential fecundity in the very race traits themselves these proportions may be altered in the long run. This is a difficult and elusive subject, which may be left to one side for the present. As far as the racial complexion of a given geographical area is concerned, this may be suddenly revolutionized by the extermination of the existing inhabitants by a group of invaders. This has probably very rarely happened in actual fact. Almost always, larger or smaller contingents of the original population survive, restricted often to the more inaccessible portions of the territory. In any case, when a number of persons of one race enter into the midst of a group of another race and carry on normal reproductive activities, the racial make-up of the latter is inevitably altered by so much. This result may take two forms. The incoming group may remain distinct, confining its matings within itself, or it may mate with the other group. In the former case, the racial make-up of the group is represented by two separate types. This is essentially the situation thus far as between the white race and the Japanese race in California. In the latter case, the result is a mixed type; this process has been at least partially carried out in the older areas of German settlement in the Northwest. In either case (with the qualification already noted) the racial outcome is determined by the relative numbers of the two types concerned.

Nationality, on the other hand, follows the lines of social transmission. By whatever means, and to whatever extent, individuals or groups can acquire the language, religion, political institutions, or any other national traits of an outside group, by those means and to that extent nationality may be altered. This means first of all that nationality may be changed without regard to the numbers of persons representing the nationalities involved. A relatively small number of people may transmit their nationality almost complete to a much larger number. This was apparently the case in the Hellenization of Greece. The Hellenes themselves seem to have been a small body of intruders from the north who brought with them into the peninsula a nationality so much more compelling than that of the natives that it rapidly became dominant over the entire people, and created one of the most brilliant epochs in human history. In the second place, it appears that nationality can be altered without any significant movement of people at all. The cultural evolution of Europe has been marked by at least two striking examples of this truth. One was the remarkable Aryan expansion, which seems to have been distinctly a cultural movement, unaccompanied, in many cases at least, by any appreciable transfer of population. Doubtless there was some original group which brought the Aryan culture to flower, and the early stages of this expansion may have been coincident with the movements of this group. But the culture itself spread with a scope and rapidity which it seems impossible to explain on the basis of population movements, especially as Aryan culture eventually became characteristic of racial groups as widely diverse as the Hindus, Greeks, Romans, Teutons, and Russians. The other example of a similar sort is furnished by the Celtic expansion. It is indicative of the possibility of complete dissociation of nationality from population movements that the particular group which is thought of to-day as distinctly Celtic — the Irish — contains very little trace of the blood of the racial group, the early Alpines or "round barrow men", with which the Celtic culture was originally associated. The nationality jumped St. George's Channel, which opposed an effective barrier to the movement of the racial group.

The outstanding fact is that race and nationality

may operate quite independently of each other. Race may change while nationality remains constant, and nationality may alter while race continues the same. One nationality may include several races, as is illustrated by Switzerland, France, the United States, and in fact many of the western countries, while on the other hand one race may include several nationalities, as is shown by the Slavic race, the Mediterranean race, and others, including the complex but definite racial blend commonly called the "Anglo-Saxon." The two references already made to Greece afford evidence of opposite possibilities. During the classical period a group of outsiders, so few in number apparently as not seriously to affect the basic racial composition of the people, brought about a radical alteration in nationality, while during practically the whole of the Christian era the Greeks have kept alive a distinct nationality in spite of a sweeping and manifold dilution of their racial stock.

Accordingly, a body of outsiders entering into a given group may produce a variety of effects upon its race and its nationality. Professor Dixon, speaking of the incursions of blond, Teutonic-speaking tribes into France and the British Isles, says, "In Britain this led to a far-reaching change of language, and profoundly influenced the physical type; in southern Germany and Austria the Teutonic invasions led also to a change of speech, but produced no lasting effect on the physical character of the people;

in France the invading Franks lost their own language, although they gave their name to the country; and although they and their kindred tribes had a more lasting effect upon the racial character of the conquered people than was the case in Germany or Austria, yet France to-day, in spite of them, forms essentially a western extension of the great central European domain of the Alpine and Palæ-Alpine peoples." [1]

Similarly the Teutonic invasions into lands farther south produced varying results. Neither the Visigoths nor the Ostrogoths remained in Italy long enough to leave any appreciable impress on the population, though the latter during their brief stay exerted such an influence on the nationality of the natives that laws had to be passed to prevent the Italians from imitating the hairdressing customs and other national traits of the invaders. But this was a transient phase, and on the whole the Goths left little more in the way of cultural monuments than of physical impress, even the type of architecture that bears their name having no direct connection with them. In the North of Italy, however, the results were different. The infiltration of Teutonic blood was large enough, continuous enough, and permanent enough to produce a lasting effect on the racial composition of the people of the region. On the other hand, the national traits, though perhaps

[1] Roland B. Dixon, "The Racial History of Man", page 59.

preserved for some time, as in the case of the Lombards, were eventually submerged by those of the natives.

There can be no general formula as to the effects of the introduction of foreign elements upon the nationality of the receiving people. It is quite a common practice among college debaters, and others more mature, to prove all dubious claims, on either side of any question, by referring to the Roman Empire. But while convenient, it can hardly be considered scientific, certainly with respect to population movements. It is the height of logical quackery to say, as is sometimes done even by persons scholarly in their own fields, "Rome succeeded in assimilating her immigrants, and I guess we needn't worry about our own." Every case of assimilation is governed by the peculiar factors which condition it, and before predicting the outcome in even the most guarded terms these factors must be fully taken into the reckoning.

And among the factors which must be taken into the reckoning are the various types of group feeling. Since, as has been observed, nationality is primarily a matter of the feelings and emotions, the effect which nationalities have upon each other when brought into contact must depend directly upon the feelings which they engender on both sides. In any such problem there are four distinct factors, which may be present in varying combinations and proportions. These are racial sympathy and racial antipathy, national sympathy and national antipathy. Both of these forms of sympathy rest upon recognized likenesses, both forms of antipathy are aroused by recognized differences. True racial feelings depend upon racial affiliations or distinctions; true national feelings upon qualities of nationality. Just as race and nationality may go together, or may follow separate pathways, so racial feelings and national feelings may be found acting harmoniously, or acting independently, or acting in opposition. This matter is of the greatest importance.

The term in commonest use in everyday conversation to include both these types of aversion, or either one of them indiscriminately, is "race prejudice." This is a phrase which has been much upon the lips of people of all nations in recent years. The frequency of its use indicates the widely recognized importance of the fundamental idea underlying it, while the looseness of its use reveals a vast amount of misunderstanding and slipshod thinking. Characteristic is the observation of Mr. H. G. Wells:

"There is no more evil thing than race prejudice. It holds more baseness and cruelty than any other error in the world."

The trouble with the customary application of the term "race prejudice" is that a very large part of what it is made to refer to is neither racial nor prejudice. Taking the latter fault first, a prejudice in the strict sense is a pre-judgment, that is, a judgment made in advance of the evidence. Now the state of mind usually alluded to is not a judgment, but a feeling, and it does not arise in advance of the evidence, but arises as a natural reaction on presentation of the evidence. The evidence consists of the traits of a person recognized to be of another race. The feeling is a feeling of revulsion or withdrawal that arises spontaneously under those conditions. It may vary in intensity and perhaps in quality according to the circumstances, that is, according to the sort of association, contact, or relationship that is involved in the meeting. The feeling of a white citizen of the United States toward a Negro varies significantly according to whether he meets him as a porter in a Pullman car, as a fellow traveler sharing his seat in that same Pullman car, or as a chance bedfellow in an overcrowded rural hotel. Brabantio could be all friendliness and hospitality to the dark-skinned warrior regaling him with stories.

"Of moving accidents by flood and field,
Of hair-breadth 'scapes i' the imminent deadly breach"

but when it came to regarding him as the husband of his daughter, that was an entirely different matter. His reaction was not a matter of judgment, certainly not of pre-judgment. It had never occurred to Brabantio to think of Othello as a possible son-in-law. But when that relationship was suddenly presented to him the mild sense of alienation which had probably always lain smoldering beneath the surface immediately flamed up into a tremendous passion.

The second respect in which the common use of the term in question is faulty is that it quite generally refers to differences which are not racial at all. The only true racial repulsion is that which is aroused by differences that are genuinely racial. As already suggested, the only racial traits that produce this effect are those which signal a difference in race to the observer. Variations in cranial index, in the composition of the blood, or in the cross section of the hair leave the average man quite cold for the simple reason that they impress him not at all. But differences in skin color, in the form or color of the hair, in the shape of the face, or in the various features of the face, when of such a nature as to indicate a difference in race, are the stimuli to true race feeling.

It is a striking fact that with reference to these observable, external race traits the white race, alone of all the great races, exhibits an extraordinary range between very wide extremes. With respect to skin color there is every gradation from the fair skin of the Swede to the coal-black skin of certain Hamites. Hair qualities vary from the waving locks of the Scandinavian "towhead" to the straight, jet-black tresses of the Italian; every degree of curliness is found short of the absolute "kink" of the Negro. Eye color varies all the way from the palest blue or gray to snapping black, stature from very tall to very short, head form from extreme dolichocephaly to pronounced brachycephaly, faces from oval or long to round or triangular, and so on through almost the entire list with the exception of certain special features like the broad nose and everted lips of the Negro. In short, it is probably safe to say that there is a much greater difference between the various types of the white race than between some of these types and any one of the other great races. To the untrained eye a Berber or Hindu Indo-European would look much more like a Negro, and an Italian would look more like an American Indian, than either would look like a typical Nordic.

There can be little doubt, therefore, that true race feeling can exist and does exist among the branches of the white race. It is said, for instance, that the Scandinavians colloquially refer to the French as "the little black men." On the other hand, it is doubtful whether race feeling always varies directly with the degree of observable external difference, or whether rather it depends upon some elusive, subconscious sense of fundamental racial differentiation. These questions are obviously difficult of determination, especially in view of the almost complete lack of scientific data, and opinions must be largely in the nature of surmise. But at least it often seems as if even the unsophisticated man had some vague inherent sense of race.

The crucial point to grasp, however, is the fact that a very large part of the aversion designated by this handy phrase is not due to racial differences at all, but to differences in language, dress, habits, food, religion, family customs, etc. It should therefore be referred to not as racial but as national. This is particularly applicable to conditions in the United States. At the present time, the average American, whatever his origin, has become so habituated to representatives of almost every variety of the white race that it is very doubtful whether there is more than an infinitesimal amount of true race antipathy felt toward any branches of the white race in this country with possibly one or two exceptions. There is abundance of aversion aroused by foreigners, we all know too well, and it is difficult to definitely isolate its causes. But it is probable that if all the cultural acquisitions of every kind could be stripped off, leaving only racial traits to judge by, there would be few barriers to association between practically all the representatives of the white race. This is evidenced by the effects of time. Give the "dirty Dago" or the "Dutch Bohunk" a generation or two to shake off the handicaps of his social and historical past, and, even though his race remain unchanged, he will slip into the American scheme of things without a ripple. If we see a tall, blue-eyed, blond giant leading up to the altar a sparkling brunette with dusky hair and darkly glowing cheeks we do not ordinarily bewail the horrible case of race miscegenation, but exclaim, "What a stunning couple!" But let a polished scion of the "upper classes" reach down among the great unwashed for his life partner, even though she be of identical racial lineage, and the community can scarce survive the shock.

All of this, be it remembered, is in pursuit of the nature of race *feeling*. The question of the social desirability of these various kinds of minglings, marital and other, is a very different, and possibly contrary, matter, to which attention will be devoted later.

To sum up, then, the common use of "race prejudice" — which is objectionable not merely for rhetorical reasons, but much more because it involves dangerously inaccurate ideas — is faulty because most of what it refers to is not racial, but national, and the remainder which is racial is not prejudice but feeling. Having made this clear, it should now be observed that there may be such a thing as genuine race prejudice, that is, an unfavorable opinion of certain foreign groups deliberately formed upon the basis of impressions conveyed by others in the form of conversations, writing, pictures, etc. This kind of actual judgment may be formed without ever coming in contact with a single representative of the foreign group. In so far as the phrase is used to refer strictly to this attitude it may be very serviceable. Mr. J. H. Oldham, in his excellent book, "Christianity and the Race Problem", follows mainly this interpretation of race prejudice, regarding this great obstacle to intergroup harmony as the product of a largely deliberate miseducation. To the extent that this is true, it would appear that if different races could only know the truth about each other race prejudice would disappear. Perhaps this may be so with reference to race prejudice. But it is not true of race antipathy. It is exceedingly doubtful if race antipathy would yield to any amount of knowledge. Mr. Oldham also raises the question whether race prejudice is inherited, and inclines to answer it in the negative. This is undoubtedly correct as applied to race prejudice itself. But it is probably inaccurate as applied to race antipathy, which includes a large part of the obstacles which Mr. Oldham really has in mind. Of course the feeling itself is not inherited; no feeling is. But it is wholly probable that the neural connections which cause a certain feeling to arise in response to a given stimulus are inherited.

Racial sympathy is manifestly the obverse of racial antipathy. The likenesses which underlie it are connected with the same traits as the unlikenesses which occasion the opposite feeling. There is a similar absence of reason, analysis, or judgment. There is the same probability of a basis in inheritance.

As a foundation for intelligent adjustment of intergroup relationships scarcely anything is more important than a correct understanding of the nature

GROUP CONTACTS

of national antipathy. As an actual factor in present-day affairs it probably ranks far ahead of racial antipathy. Here again it is hard to draw the line. But when one reflects how enormous is the influence of the barriers of language, religion, political systems, habits, customs, traditions, and national loyalty, *none of which has any necessary connection with race,* it is not difficult to be convinced that if all these obstacles could be razed, leaving only the facts of race to obstruct intergroup harmony, the task of adjustment, stupendous as it would still remain, would be reduced to m ch less than half its present proportions. A striking illustration is furnished by the existing attitude of the United States toward Russia under the Soviet government. Here is an enormous group of people, closely akin in race to the American people, with whom not so many years ago we were on terms of military alliance (or "association", to be very exact) in spite of the fact that its government was of the type that we once fought a life-and-death struggle to escape from. But to-day, because its political system has been altered to one even more repugnant to intrenched American ideas, we refrain from establishing relations with it which we would not refuse to any people on earth because of its race. The race of the Russian people has not been altered in the least. But in some important aspects its nationality has undergone a revolution. Therefore it is to us anathema.

The most summary review of the history of the past one hundred years is sufficient to show that national feeling is a much more potent force in determining group alignments than race feeling. The American people is much more closely allied in race to Germany than to France. But this did not prevent us from casting in our lot with France when we at last got ready to take a hand in determining the future of German Kultur. Many of those American citizens who are the most reluctant to receive Germany back into terms of friendship or at least toleration are themselves of distinct German race. On the other hand, less than two generations ago, when France and Germany were fighting another war, a meeting of the United States Cabinet was suspended while the members congratulated each other on the news of a great German victory. Evidence has recently been presented to show that during the Russo-Japanese War the President of the United States served notice on Germany and France that under certain conditions he would throw the weight of the United States on the side of Japan.[1] Race carried no weight whatever. The early explanation of the Great War as a struggle of "Teuton against Slav" was very soon discarded.

In short, it would probably be very difficult to trace any dominant racial factor in most of the great military alliances and antagonisms in the past few

[1] Tyler Dennett, "Roosevelt and the Russo-Japanese War", page 2.

generations. The general impression in the matter is due in large measure to misuse of the word race. The frequency with which these alignments shift indicates that there must be something much less stable than race to account for them. In point of fact, to a very large extent they have doubtless been due to the arbitrary and intricate schemes of politicians rather than to deep-seated sentiments on the part of the general populations. But the aims of the politicians, in so far as they have been genuine group aims at all, have been national aims, and the loyalty to which they have appealed to support their designs has been distinctly national loyalty, not racial. When the political unit includes several disharmonious nationalities, or when the effective government does not enjoy the natural devotion of the populace, artificial stimuli may be employed to evoke a pseudo-national feeling. It is said that in Czarist days in Russia, Jewish pogroms were sometimes initiated in order to divert the attention of the Christian people away from their grievances against the government.

The reason why nationality holds this dominant position in intergroup affairs has already been suggested. Nationality is our distinctly human endowment. Nationality makes the social environment in which each of us grows up, to which he is adapted just as the lower organism is adapted to a physical environment, and out of which one feels literally like "a fish out of water." The significance of this adaptation of the human animal to a human environment can hardly be overemphasized. How large a part it plays in the spiritual, even the physical, well-being of each of us can hardly be appreciated until one detaches himself from it for a considerable period of time. Homesickness is not due primarily to any difference in the blue of the skies, or the forms of the mountains, or even the climate itself, but to the lack of familiar social contacts and stimuli. It is the strangeness of habits, customs, sounds, smells, tastes, standards of life that causes that sinking feeling in the pit of the stomach. Most important of all, doubtless, is the unfamiliarity of speech. And this is not due solely to the difficulty of communicating ideas. Let one spend even a week, say, in an environment where he never hears the sound of his native language, even though he can converse in the speech of the land, and he will realize how vital a force in his normal existence the tones of that language are. Nostalgia may sometimes be just as acute in the midst of a group closely akin in race as in one wholly different, though a marked disparity in race, other things being equal, will probably add the final touch.

This suggests another significant consideration. The strongest possible group unity exists when national solidarity and racial identity are combined. When racial sympathy supports national sympathy group harmony reaches its maximum. No matter how well-knit the bonds of nationality, racial dissimilarity always constitutes an element of weakness in group life. The degree of this weakness depends upon the extent to which the racial differences foster active race antipathy. Thus a population composed of representatives of two or more of the main racial groups is much more unstable than one composed of subdivisions of a single main group. But it is always a risky thing for any nation, particularly a democracy, to allow racial dilution to go beyond a very limited degree. There will always be, and it is well that there should be, marked differences of opinion among the members of the most vigorous nation on matters of large public policy as well as of minor political interests. The very genius of democracy assumes the determination of these matters on their merits according to the will of the majority. But when the situation is complicated by a variety of racial allegiances there is no assurance that questions will be decided upon their intrinsic merits. It is alleged that the movement to secure an initiative law in California was complicated by a racial clash between the Japanese and the whites.[1] If this is true, it is typical of the difficulties any democracy must face which contains diverse racial elements in its electorate or even in its general population.

There naturally recurs at this point the question, previously raised, as to the extent to which intellec-

[1] John B. Trevor, "Japanese Exclusion", page 17.

tual processes, emotional responses, temperamental reactions may be racially determined. Obviously, no further answer has been found in the meantime. But perhaps it has become even clearer how tremendously important such racial features, in the measure that they actually exist, must be.

It is perhaps not superfluous to add that in the mental processes of the average individual no nice analysis is made as to the grounds of sympathy and antipathy. We like people or we do not like them. We are attracted to certain individuals and we are repelled by others. We seldom stop to ask why. As far as the members of a different group are concerned, the barrier exists in the fact that they are of a different group. That is enough. We do not need to inquire as to the grounds upon which the group differentiation rests.

It is evident, then, that when a mass of foreign population is injected into the midst of another group a number of different situations are possible. For illustration, the receiving group may be considered as a political unit. It may be a true nation like Sweden or Australia, or it may be a fortuitous aggregation held together largely by external pressure, like the old Austro-Hungarian Empire. If a nation, it may have a racially homogeneous population of either pure or mixed origin, like Australia, or it may have separate racial groups like Canada (if the definition of nation can be stretched to include Canada). Its nationality may be vigorous and inclusive, or tenuous and limited. The incoming group almost of necessity is of a different nationality from the receiving group. Racially, it may be virtually identical with the whole or with a part of the receiving population, or it may be different to a degree limited only by the diversity of the human species.

It needs no argument to show that the result of such an incursion will depend upon the particular combination of factors which exists. Before attempting to appraise further the value — or the reverse — of the figure of the melting pot it will be necessary to examine the various aspects of race and nationality as they have conditioned the immigration movement to the United States.

CHAPTER V

A NATION IN THE MAKING

OF the total number of human groups whose recognized separateness forms the basis of international problems a few have come into being within relatively very recent years. Most of these had their origin in the readjustment of social conditions which resulted from the great geographical discoveries made four or five hundred years ago. Of these, the United States is by far the most prominent. A very interesting feature about these new groups is that their development falls within the scope of reasonably reliable history, and accordingly we are in a position to know much more about their constituents and organic character than is possible with the older groups. This fact gives them an outstanding importance from the point of view of sociological research, and also enables them to analyze certain of their social problems upon a more extensive basis of fact than exists in older countries.

Accordingly in the United States the allied but contrasted problems of race and nationality may be reduced to measurably definite and tangible terms. The first element to be considered is that of race.

The human group that we refer to as the "United States", or less exactly as "America", has been built

A NATION IN THE MAKING

up from nothing since the year 1607. Its racial aspects therefore have been determined by two primary factors. The first of these is the movement of people in both directions between this and other lands, that is, migration in and out. The second is the rate at which the different elements have borne children and died, that is, natural increase. If, beginning with the moment when the first shipload of white settlers set foot on the soil of Virginia, the dwellers in this land had applied to this particular problem knowledge and intelligence that they actually possessed, it would have been possible theoretically to know exactly the elements that have gone into the composition of the American people. In other words, if record keeping in the fields of migration and vital statistics had been from the beginning as good as they are now at their best the materials would have existed for a virtually complete determination of the origins of the American people. To compile and analyze these materials would have been a task so stupendous that it might never have been practically undertaken. Nevertheless, it is interesting to speculate upon even such a remote theoretical possibility.

It should be noted at once, however, that even if complete records had been kept of the original point of departure of every single human being who has entered the territory of the United States by land or by sea, and of the parentage of every child born within the country, those facts would offer no complete solution of the racial composition of the American people. For a stream can rise no higher than its source. Even if we knew exactly from what foreign group every individual contribution to the American population had come we should know no more about the true racial composition of the American people than we know about the racial composition of those foreign groups. And to the extent that the foreign groups were mixed racially, we should know even less, for it would have been impossible to tell just what racial elements were in the body of a given migrant. The only way to be sure of the racial affiliations of a given individual is to secure his whole family tree back to Adam and Eve, unless it is definitely known that he comes from a virtually pure racial group. Now very few of the migrants to the United States have come from groups that are racially pure, and it is certainly out of the question to get the genealogy of each of them. This means that we shall probably never know exactly what the racial make-up of the American people is now, or has been at any past time. If it were possible by bodily tests to determine the exact racial affiliations of all individuals the task would be possible of achievement, provided the necessary examination could be made of every person in the population. But this is beyond the capacity of present anthropological science, in the case of mixed races.

A NATION IN THE MAKING

The best that can be hoped for in the study of the racial composition of the American people is to trace the origin of the population at any given epoch back to its sources in foreign groups. This will give at least negative results. We may be sure that there will be no racial elements represented that were not present in the groups from which the migrants came. And if the migrants are drawn uniformly from the general population of the foreign group, it may be assumed that the racial elements found in the stream of migration will be essentially the same as, and proportional to, those contained in that population as a whole. For example, the population of England is known to be of decidedly mixed race. All we know about the English colonists or immigrants, until very recent years, is that they came from England. But it is a fair assumption that in a group of one million immigrants, the proportions of early Mediterranean, Alpine, Nordic, and Semitic blood will be about the same as in the general population of England. Fortunately, this partial knowledge is very useful, if not wholly adequate, for many practical purposes. For, as already pointed out, true racial unity and identity may exist in a racially mixed group, and, as will be shown later, from the point of view of racial harmonization the country of origin is often the primary consideration.

Taking up first the factor of migration as a determinant of the racial make-up of the American people it may be convenient to divide it into two periods. The first, which may be called the "colonial" period, includes the years from 1607 to about 1783. The second, or "national" period, extends from the latter date down to the present. It may be useful to glance briefly at the kinds of information which are available as to the racial character of the streams of migration during these two periods. During the colonial period, as there was no centralized agency of control including all the settlements along the Atlantic seaboard, there could of course be no comprehensive record of arriving or departing migrants. Even the records of the local authorities are of the sketchiest possible character. If these were all we had to depend upon our knowledge of the foreign contributions to the American population would be virtually *nil*. Fortunately, some information is afforded by records of a different character, such as colonial documents of various kinds, letters, descriptions by travelers, contemporary periodicals, etc. The significance of these commentaries is increased by the fact that the colonists themselves tended to draw a sharp line between persons who came from the home State to which a particular settlement owed allegiance, and those who came from any other country. As migrants of the former type were true colonists, so those of the latter type may be considered as true immigrants; to the colonists they were known as "foreigners", a designation

A NATION IN THE MAKING 87

which was extended to include two or more generations of those who were still obviously derived from a foreign stock. Migrants from the home state, as a rule, were much more cordially welcomed than foreigners, which shows that the bonds of nationality at this time extended across the Atlantic. In an English colony, people from England were regarded as "our kind of folks" and treated as if they belonged in the colony. In a Dutch colony, people from Holland were similarly welcomed. In most of the colonies, even in Pennsylvania, the foreigner was looked upon with at least some slight trace of suspicion or hostility, and was given to understand that he was there on sufferance. Quite early the colonists recognized the dangers inherent in too great numbers of foreigners, and in some cases attempted to limit their admission by various means.

This kind of feeling evidently resulted in preserving many indications as to the origin of new arrivals which otherwise would have been lost. In the case of certain lots of newcomers which were distinguished by their size or some other unusual feature, we have quite reliable reports as to both numbers and origin. But at best, the details of this momentous movement across the Atlantic are very hazy. Certain general features, however, stand out with considerable clearness and reliability. One of these is that the actual migration, both of colonists and immigrants alike, was relatively small compared either with the total population at any time after the first few decades, or with the increase of population through the excess of native births over deaths. Benjamin Franklin stated in 1741 that a total population of about one million had been produced from a total foreign migration of less than eighty thousand. That is, the total number of outsiders who had entered the country during the hundred and thirty-four years preceding that date amounted to only about one twelfth of the population, while in 1920 the number of immigrants during only one hundred years previous amounted to about one third of the population. On the other hand, the native population was increasing at a rate unprecedented, probably, in the whole previous career of mankind upon earth. Malthus took the American colonies as an example of the extreme fecundity of which the human race is capable. In fact, the rate of increase during the whole of the colonial period was in the neighborhood of doubling every twenty years, and in some sections we are told it doubled every fifteen years, immigration being only slightly responsible for the growth. The significance of these facts is that the early settlers of such a country are of vastly greater weight in determining the character of the eventual population than an equal number of later arrivals. And we know that practically all of the earliest settlers came from England.

The second outstanding feature of migration dur-

A NATION IN THE MAKING

ing the colonial period is that during the whole of the period it came almost exclusively from Northwestern Europe, and preëminently from the British Isles. This conclusion is borne out by the various forms of evidence to which reference has been made, and is strongly confirmed by a special study of the problem made by the United States Bureau of the Census. This study is included in the volume entitled "A Century of Population Growth", and consists of a careful review of the surnames of the persons resident in the United States in 1790 and enumerated in the first Federal census which was taken in that year. A person's name, to be sure, is no final evidence as to his origin, not even as far as country is concerned and certainly not with respect to race. Nevertheless, a very strong probability is set up in the case of certain types of names, particularly at a time when surnames were more descriptive, and had not become so conventionalized as they are to-day. Thus, for example, surnames which are identical with common nouns or other parts of speech in daily use in the language of a certain country leave little room for doubt. The report in question gives a long list of typical examples of this sort which leave little room for doubt as to the nationality of those who bore them.

The following will serve as illustrations: Soup, Oyster, Fish, Trout, Salmon, Goodbread, Goodrum, Grapewine, Beer, Booze, Petticoat, Redsleeves, Highshoe, Jumpers, Overall, Iceman, Ploughman, Crook, Rascal, Blackhead, Warts, Grunts, Howls, Yells, Peacock, Commodore, Trueluck, Witchwagon, as well as some where the given name is also included, as, Peter Wentup, John Smothers, Ruth Shaves, Wanton Bump, Preserved Taft, Constant Gallneck, and so on.

At any rate, this estimate of the Census Bureau is probably the best comprehensive piece of evidence that we have as to the primary origin of the population at the beginning of our independent national life. It is summed up in the following table:[1]

Nationality	Per Cent.
English	82.1
Scotch	7.0
Irish	1.9
Dutch	2.5
French	0.6
German	5.6
All other	0.3

It will be observed at once that none of these classifications is a racial designation. The story that these figures tell as to race depends upon the racial composition of the geographical groups indicated by the names given. This will be appropriately considered a little later.

Turning now to the national period, there appears no noteworthy improvement in the records of migration — all of which, of course, is henceforth true

[1] "A Century of Population Growth", page 121.

immigration — until the year 1820. In that year the Federal Government inaugurated a series of immigration statistics which has continued down to the present. In the beginning, these were exceedingly meager, the significant information being limited practically to number, and country of origin. As time passed the kinds of information collected were greatly increased, but it was not until 1899 that positive data as to race were gathered from arriving immigrants. It is only during the past quarter of a century, therefore, that we have any authoritative material concerning the race of the foreign additions to our population. This obviously leaves the greater part of the problem untouched.

The matter of incoming foreigners is only one side — much the larger side, to be sure — of the question of the relation between migration and racial composition. The other side has to do with outgoing individuals. Just as each immigrant brings certain racial elements into the country, so each emigrant takes them out. Unfortunately, the government figures with reference to emigration date only from the year 1908. Our knowledge of the bearing of this factor upon the whole problem is therefore almost negligible. We know that there has always been a considerable outward flow from the United States to foreign countries, but we know almost nothing of the racial subtractions which it has involved.

It is all too evident, then, that practically all our positive information as to the foreign elements out of which our population has been built is limited to the countries of origin. When we turn to the question of the increase of these various elements within the United States itself the situation is even more discouraging. Positive knowledge as to the growth of the different racial elements would require a comprehensive and accurate recording of births and deaths by race all over the country. Even to-day this is very far from having been achieved. The registration area still includes only about three quarters of the total population of the country. And even within the registration area no facts are compiled as to race. Practically speaking, we have no general data as to the racial increase of our people for either the colonial or the national period.

There is one further possible source of information to which, at first thought, it might seem that we ought to be able to turn. This is the Census Reports. Every ten years we make an official accounting of our people. We began this practice, as already observed, in 1790, being almost the first country in the world to make it a regular part of government procedure. A wide variety of facts with reference to our people is secured and tabulated. It may seem surprising that the facts of race are not included in the list, but such is the case as far as the subdivisions of the white race are concerned. The nearest approach to such an attempt is found in the collection of "mother tongue" data which was initiated in the Census of 1910. But, as has already been repeatedly noted, language is no sure indication of race.

The conclusion of the whole matter is that about all we may hope ever to know about the racial makeup of the American people depends first upon what we may be able to find out with reference to the country of origin of the present stock, and second upon what we may learn as to the racial composition of the people of those countries. With reference to the former of these undertakings it is worth observing that at the time of writing the representatives of the Federal Government, in order to meet the requirements of the new immigration law, are hard at work on the problem of estimating the origin by ultimate country of birth of the total population of the United States in 1920 — a task which few statisticians are likely to envy them. Since the resources at their command are far superior to those available to the ordinary unofficial student, prudence counsels waiting patiently for the outcome of this investigation as far as the details of the question are concerned. Certain broad considerations, however, sufficient for the purposes of this study, may be set down with a reasonable degree of confidence.

The first of these is that the American people, at the beginning of its independent national existence, was to a very large extent a racial replica of the

British Isles and particularly of England. It is true that this conclusion has been vigorously attacked in recent years, but it still seems to have the great weight of the evidence on its side. At most, it is hard to see how the possible variation could be more than a few per cent. The next step, then, is to examine the racial composition of England and Wales, Scotland and Ireland. In this, as in most details of ethnography, there is no complete agreement among the experts. We must content ourselves with certain broad features which correspond to the interpretations of the majority of the specialists.

The aboriginal population of the British Isles appears to have consisted of early representatives of the great Mediterranean stock. This is a subdivision of the white race, represented to-day in nearly pure form by some of the natives of Spain and southern Italy. Its typical features are a rather low stature, normally slender build, a long head characterized, according to some students, by a distinctive pentagonal shape, a dark or olive skin, black eyes, black hair ranging from straight to wavy, a long or oval face, and a temperament variously described as emotional, excitable, passionate, mercurial, artistic, and effervescent. People belonging to a primitive branch of this race probably inhabited England in the period before the last glacial invasion. As the great ice sheet crept down over the island they were forced to retreat to the southward, but when favorable conditions were restored a population very similar in type, though probably more highly developed, reëstablished itself and proceeded to replenish the land, forming the basic population of England, Scotland, and Ireland alike. These were the so-called "long-barrow men", named from their habit of burying their dead in long earthen mounds.

Much later, but still long before the true historical period, there came from the continent a slow, pervasive drift of population of an entirely different type. These were what have been called the "round-barrow men", representing a great section of the white race for which there seems to be no better name than "Alpine." These are a short or round-headed folk, of medium stature, stocky in build, with round faces marked by high cheek bones, hair typically dark brown, eyes dark brown or gray, skin somewhat swarthy, and a disposition stolid, placid, persevering, and tractable. This is the race which carried, so far as any one race carried it, the notable Celtic culture. Moving westward from the Continent, it is natural that it should have affected first and most deeply the population of England and Wales. As has already been noted, it succeeded in crossing the Irish Sea to only a very slight degree, so that the Mediterranean character of the Irish population was very little affected. To the northward its influence was a diminishing one, extending to a certain extent into the southern portions of Scotland. These two elements composed the great bulk of the British people up to the beginning of the Christian era, though doubtless even before that time there had been some additions of the fair-skinned, light-haired stock from the north that played so prominent a part in later centuries. The period of Roman domination probably changed the racial complexion very little, partly because it involved an inconsiderable transfer of population, and partly because those who did come were a closely related Mediterranean stock.

At about the beginning of the Christian era, however, forces began to operate which in the end produced sweeping changes. These were connected with that great outpouring of humanity from the northwestern corner of Europe which occupied so important a place in the history of the continent for hundreds of years. It is not necessary for present purposes to examine the details of this movement or series of movements, or to attempt to differentiate between the various tribes or groups, however manifold the names by which they are familiarly known. From the point of view of race, Goths, Vandals, Saxons, Angles, Norsemen and Normans, Danes, Alamanni, and Franks were virtually indistinguishable. They were all sections of that remarkable "Nordic" race to which so much attention has been devoted in recent years. Whether or not it is true, as has been recently asserted, that this was itself a decidedly mixed race, the fact remains that it was a distinctive race with striking characteristics of body and mind which marked it off sharply, not only from the other great sections of the human species, but from all the other subdivisions of the white race. In stature it was tall and slender, the head and face were long, the skin fair, the eyes blue, the hair light in varying shades — the only example of light hair in the whole human family — the nose slender and straight, the temperament marked by initiative, enterprise, venturesomeness, a certain degree of phlegmatism, sometimes bordering on moroseness, and a well-developed mechanical and organizing ability.

The various steps by which successive contingents of this great stock intruded themselves into British territory are familiar to every student of history. As to the final effect upon the population of the islands there is, however, some uncertainty. We may be sure that the impression so easily gained from the accounts of the period, that the invaders virtually exterminated or eliminated the native population in the regions where they settled, is quite contrary to the facts. As already observed, the complete annihilation of a native population is almost an unknown event on any large scale. This is well illustrated in the case of the United States. In spite of the fact that the white men are customarily credited with having crowded the red men off the earth, it is estimated by competent observers that there are almost as many Indians living on the territory of the United States to-day as there were in the days of Columbus. So in England the groups that we have come to speak of as the Anglo-Saxon are to be thought of as additions rather than substitutions in the racial history of the island. Just what proportion of the final result as represented by the population of to-day, or of three hundred years ago, is to be regarded as Nordic is impossible to say with certainty. In general, the Nordic character is much more pronounced in the southern and eastern portions of Great Britain than in Wales or the north and west of Scotland where the earlier types still dominate. With respect to Ireland, there was very little infusion of Nordic blood into that island until the time of the "Great Plantation" in the early years of the seventeenth century when, under the initiative of James the First, many of the inhabitants of Scotia were moved over into the north of Ireland, laying the foundations of that remarkable stock later known as the "Scotch-Irish", and incidentally sowing the seeds of much confusion in the subsequent history of Ireland. These famous settlers, while "very little Scotch and much less Irish" were a decidedly mixed lot racially, representing most of the various elements in the British population, but with a sufficient preponderance of Nordic blood to produce a definite alteration in the stock of north Ireland.

A NATION IN THE MAKING

This is what it means, then, racially to be an "Englishman." It means that you probably have very little blood in your veins that is not Mediterranean, Alpine, or Nordic. But as to whether one or another of these stocks can claim you almost exclusively, or in what proportions they are represented in your composition, the name itself tells nothing. The situation changes, however, when it comes to dealing not with individuals, but with masses of Englishmen. Unless there is some preliminary basis of selection, it is probable that a group of thousands of Englishmen taken at random will show a distinct racial tone. All three basic stocks will be represented, but the combination will be a distinctive one, and there will be a definitely Nordic character to the whole. Accordingly, in appraising the racial character of the transatlantic movement to America during the colonial period, the term England is quite inconclusive as applied to an individual, but is profoundly significant as applied to the whole mass of population involved. Thus, if we may accept the census estimate that out of a total white population of 2,810,248 in 1790 there were 2,345,844 English we may form a reliable picture of the racial qualities of more than four fifths of the white element. We may be sure that they represented a reasonably close approximation to the population of England itself, that is, that they were Anglo-Saxon and predominantly Nordic. Furthermore, if it is true, as often asserted, that the Nordic stock is by nature venturesome, daring, and inclined to pioneering, the very fact of migration would probably exercise a selective influence, tending to accentuate the Nordic proportion among those who were willing to undertake the risks and hardships of helping to develop a new country. On this assumption, the English element in the population of the United States at the beginning of its independence would have been even more Nordic than that of England itself.

Of the non-English portions of this population it has been estimated, as already shown, that an additional 8.9 per cent. came from other parts of the British Isles, 7.0 per cent. being Scotch and 1.9 per cent. Irish. Since this estimate is based on surnames, a large part of the group called Scotch may very probably have come from the north of Ireland, where differences in religion, traditions, and group feeling might easily have preserved the original family names of the settlers for one hundred years or more. In point of fact, the Scotch-Irish constituted the largest non-English element in the total movement to America during the whole of this period. Their effect, however, upon the racial make-up of the colonial population can not have been much different from what it would have been if they had been English, for, as we have seen, their constituent elements were quite representative of the general English stock. For practical purposes, therefore, they may be included with the English. As for the small contingent set down as Irish, the maximum effect that it could have had was to increase slightly the Mediterranean element in the general composite.

The second largest group of migrants during the colonial period was composed of Germans, mostly from the Palatinate, who, with their descendants, composed 5.6 per cent. of the population of 1790. While this stock probably contained both Alpine and Nordic elements, it is reasonable to assume that the Nordic element was at least as prominent as in the English population, so that these continental additions would have altered the racial make-up of the colonial population, if at all, mainly by a slight increase in Nordic traits. The only other non-English group at this time which amounted to more than one per cent. of the total was the Dutch. They were probably more nearly pure Nordic than any other group yet considered so that their influence, also, must have been a slight accentuation of the Nordic tone. The elements of the population of 1790 derived from all other sources than those considered formed so minute a fraction as to be virtually negligible.

It appears, then, that the total population at the close of the colonial period, whether derived directly from migrants, or from the descendants of migrants, came from sources which were very nearly identical racially, or in which at least the racial composition differed in proportions rather than in nature. It is quite unlikely that there was any difference in the natural fecundity of the various basic elements sufficient to cause any significant alteration in the racial proportions of the native stock. The result was an American population composed of Nordic, Alpine, and Mediterranean elements, with the Nordic strain strongly predominant. This may be taken as the foundation of the American people. It was built up almost exclusively from northwestern European sources. Whatever racial elements there may be in southern and eastern Europe which were not represented in northwestern Europe before 1800 were not appreciable components of the original American population.

The problem of immigration to the United States, in its racial aspects, has to do with the effects of the various streams of foreign population since 1790 upon this basic population. Except for the past twenty-five years, as has already been observed, our knowledge of this matter is still based upon figures showing country of origin, not race. Though we could well wish it otherwise, there is nevertheless much light to be derived even from these unsatisfactory data.

For the first thirty years of this period no figures are available. We know, however, that it was a period of small immigration and that the sources were almost wholly the same as those of the colonial population. Accordingly, it makes little difference whether the annual immigration averaged ten thousand or twenty thousand. There was no appreciable modification of the racial constitution of the American people as a result.

Beginning with 1820 the record is complete and authentic as far as the country of origin is concerned. The data are necessarily much too extensive to be reviewed in detail in this connection. They are readily accessible to any one who cares to make the effort — which will well repay him — to look them up. For our present purposes their significance is found in certain outstanding features. The first of these is that for many decades the great bulk of the immigrants continued to come from the United Kingdom. Of these, the largest number was from Ireland, as far as the figures are conclusive. There was always a considerable number who came from the United Kingdom whose particular origin was not specified. For the first few years France came second, with Spain and Germany alternating for third and fourth places. Aside from these countries, the currents of immigration were almost negligible. As the total volume of immigration gradually increased the proportions began to change, the most striking feature being the prodigious increase of Germans. This phenomenon began to exhibit itself in 1832. Previous to that date the total immigration from Germany in a single year had never exceeded 2500.

In that year it suddenly rose to 10,194. With various fluctuations it continued to increase slowly until 1845, when an upward curve started which finally culminated in the enormous total of 215,009 in 1854. This is the largest number of Germans who ever came to us in one year, with the exception of 1882, when the total reached 250,630, and one of the largest annual contributions from any country at any time. At just about the same time the immigration from Ireland was soaring to even higher figures. In the year 1851 it reached the total of 221,253, and its aggregate for a period of about ten years far exceeded that from Germany. In the later period, centering about the year 1882, however, the Irish immigration fell considerably short of the German, and for the whole period of recorded immigration the Germans hold the lead, not only over the Irish but over all other immigration currents. A total of 5,568,702 Germans came to the United States between the years 1820 and 1923 as against 8,430,777 from the entire United Kingdom.

The only other source of immigration which attained a noteworthy position previous to 1882 was the Scandinavian countries. The current from this source increased slowly but remained inconsiderable until about 1879 when it suddenly began to mount, and held a prominent place for the next fifteen or twenty years, though the total never approached that of Germany or Ireland. During the period 1820 to

1923, there were 2,219,522 immigrant arrivals from Sweden, Norway, and Denmark.

Up to 1882, these three sources — the United Kingdom, Germany, and the Scandinavian countries — contributed almost the entire bulk of the immigration to the United States. Minor contingents came from France and Switzerland, and of course there were scattered representatives from most of the countries of the world. From the racial point of view, it is easy to see, the effects upon the American population were of little significance. No new elements were brought in, and the relative proportions of the different basic stocks were probably little altered. While the Irish were more nearly pure Mediterranean than the average of the American people, the Scandinavians certainly, and the Germans probably, were more distinctly Nordic, so that the final result was probably little more than a slight diminution in the Alpine proportion.

In a general way, then, it may be said that the immigration problem in the United States was not a racial problem previous to the year 1882. The result of immigration was to rebuild on American soil out of the same basic elements the particular type of composite population which had furnished the original settlers, and which had maintained itself as the preponderant stock in the native population from the very beginning. It is consequently very doubtful if true racial antipathy played any appreciable part in the sentiment of the American people toward immigration during the first one hundred years of our national life. There was opposition and criticism in plenty, as is well known, but it rested almost entirely upon other than racial grounds. Possibly the fact that the Irish and the Scandinavians were more nearly of a single race than the average American may have occasioned some slight sense of racial alienation, but it can not have exerted more than an infinitesimal influence.

CHAPTER VI

A NEW MENACE

BEGINNING about 1882, however, a marked change in the situation began to develop. Certain new streams of immigration, which had hitherto trickled in almost unnoticed, began to swell to portentous proportions. Foremost among these were the currents from Italy, Austria-Hungary, and the Russian Empire and Finland. Streams smaller in proportion but of immense volume in the total came from various of the Balkan states, Portugal, Turkey, Greece, etc. Even after they began to increase these currents remained below the older ones for a number of years. Italy, which had never sent more than nine thousand before 1880, in that year raised its contribution to over 12,000, and in 1882 sent 32,159, a very considerable body of people, but quite trifling compared with the delegations from the United Kingdom and Germany. The movement from Austria-Hungary, previous to 1880, had reached about the same maximum as that from Italy, but in that year it rose to over 17,000 and two years later to over 29,000. The Russian Empire still lagged behind, sending only 16,918 in 1882.

It is not necessary for present purposes to make a detailed inquiry into the causes of the sudden expansion of these streams. The development of transportation facilities by land and water, the spread of popular education and geographical knowledge, the extending reputation of the United States as the land of promise, and the gradual development of a spirit of independence and initiative among the peasants of southern and eastern Europe all played their part. The important fact is that, having once received the impetus, these streams continued to grow until, in a very short time, they dominated the situation. As the "new immigration" increased the "old immigration" diminished, not only relatively but absolutely. The records set by the United Kingdom, Germany, and the Scandinavian countries were never equaled again. The definite turn of the balance came about the year 1896. From that time on until the outbreak of the Great War a larger and larger majority of the total flow was claimed by the new immigration. In 1914 the old immigration amounted to only 13.6 per cent. of the entire number. It seems evident that forces were at work which, if they had not been interrupted by the War, would in a few years have reduced the old immigration almost to zero.

The question of immediate interest is: What was the racial significance of this radical change in the sources of immigration? Were the immigrants of the past generation simply continuing to rebuild the American population along the original lines? Were

A NEW MENACE

they notably altering the proportions of the racial composite? Were they introducing some entirely new elements? The answer to these questions is to be found in the racial composition of the people of the countries of southern and eastern Europe, a most baffling field of investigation, to be sure.

The outstanding feature of the racial situation in these lands is the very small proportion of Nordic blood represented in their populations. This by itself means that immigration from these sources tends inevitably to reduce the Nordic proportion in the American population. In its place will be substituted primarily Mediterranean and Alpine elements. Taking Italy first, we find that there is a distinct difference in the racial color of the northern and southern portions of the kingdom. In the south, the population is still preponderantly Mediterranean, in Sicily and Sardinia reaching a degree of purity probably as great as is to be found in any large area in Europe. In the north, on the contrary, there is a very large admixture of both Alpine and Nordic. If the Italian immigration to the United States had come from northern Italy its racial effect on the American population would have been relatively slight. In point of fact, the very great bulk of it came from southern Italy, the northerners preferring to go to the South American countries. In Spain and Portugal the racial preponderance is distinctly Mediterranean, with probably a considerable negroid admixture in some regions. In the old Austro-Hungarian Empire a conglomerate mass of races was artificially bound together. The prevailing elements, however, were mainly of the Alpine stock. This is true to even a greater extent with reference to the Balkan States taken as a whole. The population of Russia, ordinarily spoken of as Slavic, seems to contain a considerable Nordic element in its northwestern branches, as evidenced by the light color of the hair and eyes. There is reason to believe that the Nordic race first began its distinctive development in this general region, so that the present existence of this type may be due to a continuous preservation of the stock as well as to expansion from the west at a later date. For the rest, the population of western Russia, from which our immigrants have mostly come, is mainly Alpine.

It appears, then, that the first effect of the immigration from eastern Europe was to increase the Alpine proportion in our population. This would have been an important fact in itself. But more was involved than that. Eastern and southeastern Europe have been the scene of a long series of invasions, coming in general from the east. The best known of these, probably, because the most spectacular, is that of the Huns, but there were several others much more fateful as regards the racial make-up of the region than the Huns. Prominent among these are the Avars, the Bulgars, the Magyars, and

A NEW MENACE

the Turks. Without attempting to go into the complicated and somewhat obscure history of these movements, it appears that many if not most of them had their origin in that remarkable Turki or Tatar stock which has contributed out of its abundant fecundity to the population of so many remote regions. This stock appears to be essentially Mongoloid in its racial affiliations, so that the lands which were the immediate sufferers from these invasions must have received important permanent additions of Mongoloid stock, however effectively the fact may be concealed by the processes of race mixture, and the modification of cultures. It follows that immigration from these regions has the effect of introducing into the American population considerable strains of Mongoloid germ plasm, just how extensive no one can tell, but certainly sufficient to be of great importance.

A further factor to be considered in connection with the new immigration is the Hebrews. To just what extent the Hebrews are to be considered a race it is impossible to say. There is a marked difference of opinion, not only on the part of non-Hebrew students, but also of many leaders of Hebrew thought. Their remarkable combination of culture and religion, or culture dominated by religion, with its restrictions and prescriptions, and their remarkable faithfulness to these restrictions have perpetuated a degree of inbreeding which has kept them related in kin to an extraordinary extent in view of all their manifold wanderings and vicissitudes. Yet it is inconceivable that in the course of all these wanderings and residence in various lands, there should have been no admixture of blood, and it seems quite certain that at times numerous outside groups have been Judaized as a whole. One thing, at least, is sure; the great bulk of Hebrew immigration in recent years has been from eastern Europe, so that if it is not actually a separate race, it is definitely affiliated with the new immigration.

The conclusion is that, beginning about 1882, the immigration problem in the United States has become increasingly a racial problem in two distinct ways, first by altering profoundly the Nordic predominance in the American population, and second by introducing various new elements which, while of uncertain volume, are so radically different from any of the old ingredients that even small quantities are deeply significant. A somewhat vague, but widespread and rapidly growing popular appreciation of this fact contributed largely to the general support of the immigration law of 1924.

A new problem of group unification, therefore, was created by the typical immigration of the last generation. Instead of facing national complications alone, the United States was confronted with the additional problem of race mixture. To get even a partial idea of all that this involved it is nec-

A NEW MENACE

essary to consider in some detail what the nature of race mixture is, and what results may be expected to follow when numbers of persons representing two or more different racial stocks are put in close territorial contact with each other.

We have observed that the qualities of race are carried in the germ plasm; that in a given stream of germ plasm they remain constant and unchanged from generation to generation; and that the only way they are modified is by putting them together in different combinations. The basic elements are never changed. It follows that, no matter how closely associated representatives of different races may be, there will be no change in the racial characteristics of any of them unless physical matings take place. Social contacts and associations alone, even though continued over many generations, will produce no alteration in racial qualities. If there had been no physical matings between whites and Negroes from the time when the first shipload of African slaves was landed in Virginia in 1619 down to the present moment, the descendants of those first "involuntary immigrants" and of all the later consignments would to-day be of exactly the same racial type as their ancestors were when they came and as their kinsmen are in the jungles of Africa to-day. No amount of intimate social association would have modified a single black or a single white toward the opposite type. This is equally true of representatives of races less widely separated than the Negroes and the whites; it is true of all divisions that are truly racial.

The question then is, under what conditions do matings take place among associated racial groups, and what is the character of the products of those matings? The answer to the first part of this question is that some matings will take place under almost any conceivable conditions. Doctor Harry H. Laughlin, in a statement before the House Committee on Immigration and Naturalization, summed the matter up in the following words: "The committee of the Eugenics Research Association has had the matter in hand, and has failed to find a case in history in which two races have lived side by side for a number of generations and have maintained racial purity. Indeed, you can almost lay it down as an essential principle that race mixture takes place whenever there is racial contact."[1] The reasons for this are obvious. As has been observed, the prevailing opinion among scientists is that all races of men are descended from a single original stock, and are still to be considered as belonging to a single species. At any rate, all existing data seem to indicate that fertile unions are possible among all human races, and that the sexual impulse knows no racial boundaries.

---

[1] Biological Aspects of Immigration, Sixty-Sixth Congress, Second Session, April 16-17, 1920, page 15.

The last statement requires some examination and possible qualification. The factor of racial antipathy has to be taken into consideration. When sexual attraction and racial repulsion are brought into conflict the outcome may be dubious. It probably differs with different individuals, according to the relative strength of the two motives in each particular case. With reference to those legitimate forms of mating, represented by sanctioned wedlock, there is of course no uncertainty. Racial antipathy is a powerful barrier to marriage, and therefore a notable check on racial mixture, since in every society the offspring born in wedlock far exceed those born outside. But after all, marriage is an institution, and therefore belongs in the category of national factors, not racial. Unless racial antipathy is so strong as to prevent not only marriage, but also all matings outside of wedlock on the part of all individuals of diverse race, there will be some race mixture. The existence of the large mulatto class in the United States is sufficient evidence that the potency of racial antipathy falls far short of this complete barrier, even in a supposedly highly civilized community and even between races that represent almost the extremes of diversity. As obvious racial differentiations diminish, the effect of race feeling in even checking interbreeding diminishes likewise, until, as already observed, in such a country as the United States, it becomes almost a negligible factor as far as the various sections of the white race are concerned.

It follows that a country receiving large contingents of foreigners of different races, especially if they are not too widely separated, need have no doubt as to the processes of race mixture — they will go on spontaneously without encouragement, and in spite of impediments. To the extent to which they are retarded — which may, to be sure, be a very important extent — the causes are to be found more in national feeling than in racial feeling. This will be considered later. What such a country really needs to concern itself about is the effects of race mixture. This is a profoundly important problem concerning which, unfortunately, it is as yet impossible to state conclusions with certainty. The difficulties of carrying on experiments with human beings, and the scanty information that exists with reference to the "natural experiments" which have taken place at various times and places, leave the question as to the final effect of the mixing of human races quite unsettled. For our tentative conclusions we are forced to rely very largely upon the analogies furnished by experiments and observations upon the lower animals and plants. Fortunately, these are analogies in which we may place a high degree of confidence. For, as already repeatedly emphasized, race mixture is strictly a biological process, and in his biological processes man is closely

A NEW MENACE

akin to other types of living organisms. This is particularly striking in matters pertaining to reproduction, in which certain general principles run through all species, down almost to the very lowest forms. It is reasonable to assume, therefore, that facts of heredity which are universal, at least in the higher forms of animal life, will be carried over into the human field.

From the point of view of the transmission and inheritance of definite traits, the significant fact is that the germ plasm contains an enormous multitude of small particles, called "genes" or "determiners", the capacity and function of which is to cause the appearance of certain particular traits in the body of the individual. For each separate trait there is a particular determiner which may be present singly or doubly. The determiners never combine or fuse, but maintain a continuous and independent succession through unlimited generations of the species. As a result, each separate trait is inherited independently. The human body, therefore, may be thought of as a sort of mosaic, composed of a multitude of separate traits, each due to the presence of a particular type of determiner in one or the other, or both, of the two germ cells out of the union of which it has grown. Practically speaking, half of the determiners come from the mother and half from the father. Half of those which come from the mother, or one quarter of the total, are derived from the maternal grandfather, and half from the maternal grandmother; half of those from the father are derived from the paternal grandfather and half from the paternal grandmother. And so on in multiples of two back through indefinite generations of ancestry.

If we can imagine the mating of two persons of absolutely pure stock of different races, each of the offspring would receive half of its determiners from the germ plasm of one race and the other half from the germ plasm of the other race. In other words, they would all be strictly half-breeds. It does not follow that in appearance they would be an exact mean in all particulars between the two original types. Sometimes one determiner of a given type is dominant over the other determiner and so the bodily trait corresponding to that type of determiner shows a greater resemblance to one parent than to the other. But in the germ plasm which is passed on to the next generation the determiners remain evenly divided between the two racial sources. When we come to consider the mating of mixed races the outcome is by no means so simple. Various combinations are possible in the offspring. The significant fact is that out of thousands of matings between representatives of different racial stocks, whether pure or mixed, the offspring as a whole will in the long run display the characteristic features of all the different races in approximately the same proportions that they occurred in the total group of parents.

A NEW MENACE

The phrase "race mixture" then, unlike so many popular phrases, accurately describes the process to which it is commonly applied. The product of the mating of different racial stocks really is a mixture. It may be compared to pouring together various chemically inert liquids — water, milk, wine, ink, etc. If the resulting mixture is thoroughly stirred, it will have the appearance of a smooth homogeneous liquid. But every separate molecule remains just what it was before the mixing took place; there is just as much water, just as much milk, just as much wine, just as much ink, as there was at the beginning. The analogy with race mixture is particularly close if some of the ingredients — like milk, for instance — are themselves mixtures, corresponding to mixed races.

It will be obvious at once that in this respect the analogy of the melting pot itself is not far amiss. The fusion that takes place within a crucible, assuming that there is no true chemical action, is not unlike the process of race mixture. The product is a molecular mosaic, just as the human body is a mosaic of separate racial traits. If the problem to which the figure of the melting pot was applied had been simply the question as to whether race mixture could and would take place in the United States as a result of indiscriminate immigration there would have been little to criticize. In fact, it was vastly more than that. The symbol of the melting pot was pitiably inadequate in the first place because, as we shall see later, the major part of the problem had nothing to do with race mixture, and, in the second place, because it confined itself exclusively to the *process*, and gave no heed to the *result*. And the result is the really important consideration.

A melting pot is not an end in itself. The purpose of a melting pot is to get heterogeneous substances into a form of unity and fluidity. But two great questions remain: What kind of a substance are you going to have when the fusion is complete? And what are you going to do with it?

Taking the latter of these queries first, it has been aptly observed that a melting pot implies a mold. The object in fusing the various ingredients is to get them into a plastic state so that they may be cast into a predetermined form which they will thereafter retain permanently. In this respect the analogy of the melting pot as applied to races in America obviously breaks down completely. The assumption is that the mixture itself is the final goal; there is nothing even remotely corresponding to a mold into which it is to be poured.

Much more important than this, however, is the question as to the character of the mixture itself. On this point, the champions of racial amalgamation for the most part beg the question. They seem to assume that if it can be proved that racial fusion will eventually be complete, that settles the

A NEW MENACE

matter. Nothing more need be said. They ignore the consideration as to whether the molten mass will be good for anything. True, certain sweeping statements are made to the effect that mixed races are superior to either of the originals, especially if the latter are not too far apart, and some efforts are made to bolster up this assertion by reference to various of the great civilizations of history. But these are mostly *ex cathedra* pronouncements, without a semblance of support by any factual evidence. It is, indeed, as already stated, a matter about which we know very little. The various cases of race mixture about which information is available are so complicated by social and environmental factors, often of a very unfavorable kind — as, for instance, in the case of the racial nondescripts in the seaports of the world — that it is practically impossible to isolate the results of purely racial factors. Consequently, it is easy to assert that the environmental factors are the ones responsible for the poor results, and that if these racial crosses had been given half a chance they would have been at least the equals of either of their parents.

Here, again, biology fortunately comes to our aid. The mixing of races among plants and animals has been carried on to a very vast extent, and many definite principles and rules have been worked out. Only the simplest and most fundamental need concern us here. First of all it should be recognized that many of the most beautiful, most useful, and generally finest types of plants and animals are crosses. The crossing of races is not necessarily disastrous. But these desirable crosses are either the result of long experimentation with various combinations or else of the union of carefully selected varieties chosen deliberately for certain traits which they possess and which promise to blend to advantage. No breeder would expect to improve his stock by random crossing with any variety that chanced to present itself. In other words, the desirable crosses are just as definite in their racial composition as the pure varieties.

More than this, the plant or animal breeder knows that the indiscriminate mixing of a large number of varieties can be expected to produce just one result — the mongrel. This is true even though the different varieties themselves may each be of a high type. The reason for this is clear. As remarked above, the germ plasm carried by every individual contains two classes of genes, first, those that are common to all the members of his species and give him the characteristic features of his species, and second, those that are peculiar to his own variety or race, and mark him off as a member of that particular kin-group. The varieties of the various species have been produced by specialization in the germ plasm. In wild plants and animals this specialization is produced by the general processes of natural

A NEW MENACE

selection; in domesticated creatures it is the result of the manipulations of the breeder, usually with a definite type or program in mind; and in man it is the outcome of the processes of race formation which have already been discussed. Accordingly, when a large number of different varieties are bred together the tendency is for the specialized genes to neutralize or cancel each other, and for the common general genes to support each other and intensify the corresponding qualities. The result to be looked for in the offspring is therefore a primitive, generalized type — often spoken of as a "reversion", "atavism", or "throwback."

There is every reason to believe that these rules hold good for man in his biological aspects. Many mixtures of human races have taken place, and some of them seem to have not only definite traits, but desirable traits according to certain widely accepted criteria. The combination of a large amount of Nordic with smaller proportions of Mediterranean and Alpine has certainly produced a type with outstanding characteristics; in the judgment of many persons (specifically those who are members of it) it is a type of peculiar excellence. This is the English type and it is the American type. It remained the prevailing type of the immigrants to America up till nearly the close of the nineteenth century. It is certainly a notable type, with a remarkable record of achievement in the past and promise of achievement for the future. Whether one likes the type or not, it is at least a known quantity. And it is a highly specialized type.

The change in the character of immigration which developed within the past generation and a half signalized the beginning of the process of mongrelization of this type. This process was not nearly so extreme in degree or rapid in rate as it would have been if we had not definitely excluded, by various means, the Chinese, Japanese, and Hindus as soon as their respective numbers began to reach serious proportions, and if the immigration of Negroes and Malays had not been negligible in proportions for reasons which need not delay us here. Nevertheless, the new arrivals were sufficiently different, not only in their racial proportions but in their basic elements, to threaten the existing type with annihilation. What the resulting product would have been at the end of two centuries can not be definitely determined, nor can it be positively asserted that it would have been inferior to the present type. The latter is largely a matter of taste. It is almost certain that it would have been a much less specialized type, resembling much more closely a more primitive stage of human evolution. If any one, contemplating this probability, is led to deplore the check to such a development he is of course fully entitled to his own views.

It should be emphasized that this process of mongrelization takes place regardless of whether or not the component elements are of a high type. If we must have a symbol for race mixture, much more accurate than the figure of the melting pot is the figure of the village pound. If one can imagine a pound from which no dog was ever rescued, and in which all the denizens were free to interbreed at will, and into which dogs of every variety were introduced continuously for many dog generations, he will have an excellent representation of the racial situation of a country which receives all races of immigrants indiscriminately. The population of the pound, after a few generations, would be composed, aside from the newcomers, exclusively of mongrels. And this would be true even though none but thoroughbreds — Airedales, Greyhounds, Chows, Pekinese, Cockers, Doberman-Pintschers, etc. — had been placed within its confines. Mongrelization implies no inferiority on the part of the original constituents. So in a human society the prediction of a mongrel population as the almost certain product of a free-for-all immigration policy carries no more slur against the foreign elements than against the natives. It simply means a loss of specialization on all sides.

Now whether this loss of specialization, or mongrelization, among human stocks is a thing to be desired or a thing to be shunned is a matter partly of knowledge, partly of judgment, partly of taste. There is certainly a good deal to be said for the mongrel. As a canine, he is tough, resourceful, and remarkably able to take care of himself. It may be that as a human he would display corresponding features. According to the New York *Times:* [1]

"Dr. Henry Fairfield Osborn, who presides over the American Museum of Natural History, extols the wholesome boyhood of the caveman. He figures, in effect, that old Peter Cro-Magnon's son had a better preparation for life than, say, J. Bleeker Knickerbocker's child, now at Princeton."

While this, being a matter of environment, has nothing to do directly with race, there may be those who believe that by native qualities themselves the Cro-Magnon youngster, and his father as well, were better equipped to cope with difficult situations than their highly specialized descendants, and that if modern man, having achieved an extraordinarily efficient economic culture, could now reduce his own internal mechanism to a simpler and more primitive form, he would be more able to get some real comfort out of life.

But few dog lovers regard the mongrel as the most admirable product of canine evolution, and few members of any of the more highly specialized human groups are likely to look with favor upon the submergence of the distinctive traits of their stock beneath a flood of Cro-Magnon or Neanderthal humanity. At any rate there is this to be said: Whatever

[1] March 29, 1925, Section 9, page 2.

the qualities of the races of to-day may be, good or bad, they are at least known. The qualities of a future composite race are not known. It is conceivable that they might be good. But it is also wholly possible that they might be very bad. It is a very widespread, and probably salutary, human trait that

> makes us rather bear those ills we have
> Than fly to others that we know not of.

Furthermore, in this respect it is never too late to mend. If the progress of future scientific research should establish the fact that indiscriminate race mixing is desirable, or that certain definite crosses can be depended upon to produce good results, it would be relatively easy by deliberate social policies to promote whatever combinations the evidence called for. But, on the other hand, if racial mixture is actually allowed to take place, and then the results are found to be undesirable, it is virtually impossible to correct the mistake. The false steps could not be retraced. It is as impossible to unmix races as to unscramble the proverbial egg. This whole matter of race mixture seems to be one where it is quite legitimate to apply the good old maxim, "In case of doubt, don't."

It is probably an evidence of the sound judgment of democracies, to which reference has already been made, that the people of the United States, by successive steps, have expressed their determination to keep the racial tone of the population about what it was at the time of the Declaration of Independence. Each time that the threat of dilution by a widely different race has appeared it has been met decisively. The first instance was furnished by the Chinese immigration, which began to assume noteworthy proportions soon after the middle of the last century. At first these quaint, exotic strangers received a hearty welcome. They filled a useful place in the womanless organization of the mining camps. But as their numbers increased the sentiment rapidly changed, and a demand for their total debarment arose which eventually culminated in the Chinese Exclusion Acts. The next widely different race to present itself was the Japanese. Exactly the same psychological development took place. A primary attitude of welcome on the part of the American people rapidly gave place to bitter opposition as the numbers of immigrants increased, and in the end the movement was virtually stopped by means of the famous Gentlemen's Agreement. At about the same time a rising current of Hindus was checked, first by a severe interpretation of the general immigration law, by which every Hindu was assumed to be either a polygamist or likely to become a public charge, or both, and later, in 1917, by the "geographical delimitation clause", which marks out an arbitrarily bounded "barred zone", including large

A NEW MENACE

sections of Asia and most of the South Sea Islands from which no immigrants are permitted to come. Thus before the end of the Great War immigration to the United States had been definitely restricted, practically speaking, to the white and African races. This is an incongruous and anomalous combination, the *raison d'être* of which is to be found in the history of the Negroes in this country. In point of fact, there has never been more than a very small immigration of African blacks. If this current had ever reached conspicuous proportions there is little doubt that some effective means would have been discovered and applied to check it.

It must be confessed that the means by which the non-white races have been excluded, and the character of much of the popular agitation in the matter, leave much to be desired. But bad means, contrary to many pious platitudes, not infrequently produce good results, and there can be no doubt that the policy of keeping this as far as possible a white man's country is fully justified in the event. At least, the native citizen of the older American stock finds it difficult to think without a shudder of what the situation would be in this country to-day if there had been no check to Oriental immigration for the past one hundred years.

The outstanding feature of the post-War sentiment of the American people was the conviction that the mere exclusion of the non-white races did not go far enough in racial discrimination. It was more and more strongly felt that there must also be some definite measures to check any further dilution of the typical American mixture, any alteration in the basic proportions of the various sections of the white race. It was realized that while there is not in any accurate sense an "American race", the components of the American people are decidedly limited in variety, and combined in characteristic proportions, and that this racial composite must be held largely responsible for the development of an American culture distinctly agreeable at least to Americans. The destruction of this characteristic racial foundation held potentialities of change in American institutions and cultural values which the bulk of the citizens did not care to face. A detailed examination into the causes of this alteration in attitude would take us too far afield. The War itself doubtless had a great deal to do with it. The bright searchlight which the great conflict turned upon social relations threw into bold relief the truth of many obscure problems. Probably the continued insistence of the special students of the question had its effect upon public opinion, bringing, among other things, a better comprehension of the real nature of racial factors. Whatever the causes, the fact is that racial considerations played a wholly unprecedented part in the post-War agitation about immigration. The popular voice demanded not only a positive reduction in the total volume of immigration, but a reapportionment of such immigration as there was so as to bring the "old immigration" once more into predominance, that is, to provide that immigration, however voluminous, should leave the racial proportions of the American people intact.

In seeking to meet this demand, Congress, most of the influential members of which were already thoroughly persuaded, adopted a device which had been suggested many years before, and which has now become widely familiar as the "percentage" or "quota" plan. This idea, as embodied in temporary legislation which ran for three years, provided that the total immigration of persons of a given nationality in any fiscal year should be limited to three per cent. of the foreign-born persons of that nationality who were resident in the United States in 1910, as reported by the census of that year. The question will probably at once arise, why, if this legislation was a response to a demand for racial discrimination, was it expressed in terms of nationality? The answer is simple. As has already been shown, our actual knowledge of the racial composition of the American people, to say nothing of the various foreign groups, is so utterly inadequate that the attempt to use it as a basis of legislation would have led to endless confusion and intolerable litigation. So Congress substituted the term nationality, and defined nationality as country of birth. It is clear, then, that "nationality", as used in this connection, does not conform exactly to the correct definition of either nationality or race. But in effect it affords a rough approximation to the racial character of the different immigrant streams. Certainly it had the result of drawing the great bulk of our immigration once more from those countries out of which our original population had been built up.

This discriminatory effect of the quota principle was due to the fact that the old immigration, though coming in only small numbers in recent years, had been coming for so long that it had built up large reservoirs of foreign-born population by 1910, while the new immigration, though of enormous volume in the two decades just before the census of 1910, had been coming for so short a time that its base numbers were small. Thus a three per cent. quota admitted considerably more immigrants from northwestern Europe than had actually been coming in recent years, but only a fraction of those from southern and eastern Europe.

By the time Congress was ready to put the principle of restriction in permanent form in 1924, advanced thought on the question had reached the point where it was recognized that quotas based on foreign-born residents exclusively were illogical and themselves discriminatory against the old stock. It was realized that the native population had at least as good a right as foreigners to be considered in determining the composition of the immigration of the future. If the goal was to preserve the racial character of the American people, why not go at it directly? The proposal was therefore made that instead of quotas based on foreign-born residents there should be a flat total of one hundred fifty thousand set for the quota countries, and that this total should be distributed among the quota countries in the same proportions as persons deriving their origin from each country respectively were found among the residents of the United States by the census of 1920. This is called the principle of "national origins", nationality once more being defined as country of birth. The task, then, is to make an estimate of the foreign sources of the total population of the country, clear back to the first white settlements, and to express this estimate in terms of the proportions of the population of 1920 attributable to each foreign country respectively. The annual total of one hundred fifty thousand is to be apportioned pro rata. In order that time might be allowed for the making of this estimate it was provided that this plan should not go into effect for three years, that is until the fiscal year beginning July 1, 1927. In the meantime, the old quota plan is continued, the percentage, however, being reduced to two, and the census of 1910 being replaced by that of 1890, which obviously has the effect of prodigiously favoring the old immigration, as it was meant that it should.

All of these provisions apply only to the Eastern Hemisphere. The countries of both of the American continents and the adjacent islands are at present left without numerical restriction at all. This plainly leaves a large loophole for racial admixture in the future. It also seems to convey a peculiar implication as to the relative desirability of the peoples of Mexico and the West Indies, for instance, and those of Italy or Roumania. Of course the fact is that something more than racial considerations led to the decision to exempt our neighbor countries from quantitative regulation. Nevertheless, the possibilities of serious race mixture involved in a heavy migration from the regions to the south of us are so great that there has already developed a vigorous sentiment in favor of bringing all countries under some form of quota regulation, and it is wholly probable that the next few years will see a definite maximum fixed to the migration of persons of every nationality.

As far as we can look into the future, then, it appears that the race problem in the United States will be confined to the unification of the various elements already established here. Further additions represented by the immigration of the future will involve few complications of a truly racial character. With reference to the sections of the white race already included in the American population, there is little doubt that the process of unification by amalgamation will go on steadily and irresistibly, until at the end of a few generations racial differentiation will have been practically wiped out, and the population of the country will once more present a racially homogeneous aspect. And we may hope that, diverse as the present varieties may be, the proportions of the definitely esoteric elements are sufficiently small so that the degree of resulting mongrelization will not be enough to reduce seriously the racial effectiveness of the American people.

CHAPTER VII

THE MEANING OF ASSIMILATION

IF the problem of group unification created by the immigration movement to the United States had been exclusively a racial one, we could sum up the matter by saying that, having been confronted with a succession of menacing situations, we have met them one after another by measures the effect of which is to preserve this country first of all as a white man's country, and second as a country inhabited by persons belonging to that particular mixture of white racial elements which we commonly refer to as "English" or now as "American."

But the racial disintegration implied in unregulated immigration is only a part — and much the smaller part — of the total danger. The most significant unity of the American people is national unity, and the outstanding problem involved in immigration has been the problem of preserving national unity in the face of the influx of hordes of persons of scores of different nationalities. The process by which a nationality preserves its unity while admitting representatives of outside nationalities is properly termed "assimilation" and this process now demands consideration.

THE MEANING OF ASSIMILATION

On reflection, it becomes clear that assimilation, as applied to social affairs, is itself a figure of speech or symbol, but one which has been in use so long that its analogical origin has been obscured. The idea of assimilation is plainly taken from the metabolic processes of living organisms, and implies the conception of society as akin to an organism. As Herbert Spencer so cleverly demonstrated in that famous comparison in which he seems to be trying to make the reader believe — what he really does not believe himself — that society actually is an organism, there is sufficient resemblance between the organic structure of a society and that of a living creature to furnish many very illuminating suggestions as to social processes, drawn from the study of animate forms, provided the safeguard is always maintained of remembering that it is, after all, only an analogy. This is particularly true in the matter of assimilation.

In the case of an organic being, assimilation is a part of the nutritive process. The process as a whole consists in taking into the body various extrinsic substances, subjecting them within the body to certain transforming forces by which they are reduced to uniformity, and then incorporating this uniform matter into the very body of the organism. As the content of the word itself suggests, the portion of this process included in the idea of assimilation is the process of transformation, the changing of the heterogeneous into the homogeneous, the unlike to the like.

In this process there are several features of remarkable utility in promoting an understanding of the nature of social assimilation. In the first place, no organism — not even an ostrich — has the capacity of achieving the necessary transformation in the case of every conceivable kind of external object. Only certain types of substances will respond to the assimilative agencies in the body of any given organism, and the wise organism will see to it that other substances are not admitted except in strictly limited quantities. There is also a difference in the readiness with which assimilable substances yield to treatment. Those which are especially resistant can be taken less often and in smaller quantities than the opposite type. In the second place, even appropriate substances can not undergo the process of assimilation except as they come in contact with those organs of the body which are endowed with assimilating power, and under conditions which promote assimilation. In the third place — and this, as we shall see, is perhaps most significant of all — the final destiny of all assimilated material is to be transformed into the particular kinds of cells of which the organism is composed and eventually to be incorporated into the body of the organism itself. All trace of diverse origin is completely lost. If it be, for instance, a human organism, there is no suggestion that certain cells have originated in a slice of beefsteak, others in a cut of mince pie, and still

THE MEANING OF ASSIMILATION

others in a plate of pistachio ice cream. They have all become human cells. Nor do assimilated materials of a given origin arrange themselves in definite locations in the body, preserving an independent and separate identity. Neither the foot, nor the hand, nor the eye says, "I am not of the body." There is one common type to which all the assimilated materials conform,— that of the body itself. In the fourth place, the organism undergoes no change to correspond to the different sources from which its food substances come. Different substances doubtless play somewhat different rôles in the bodily economy, but because a human being has eaten sugar there is no tendency for his cells to take on a resemblance to those of the sugar cane, nor because he eats chicken does he therefore become like a fowl. Finally, in order that the assimilative processes may take place, the organism itself must be sound, healthy, and well organized.

The application of these elemental facts to the processes of social assimilation has doubtless already suggested itself. As remarked above, the analogy is remarkably close. The assimilating body is an organization, not an organism, but with striking resemblances to a true organism. It is a society — in the present sense a society of the type defined as a nation. Into this body are received extraneous elements, foreign individuals, persons of a different nationality. It is axiomatic that as long as these differences persist unity is diminished by just so much, and that if unity is to be restored, these differences must be harmonized in some way.

There are three conceivable methods or processes whereby a nation may maintain its unity in the face of constant incoming streams of persons of other nationalities. The first is symbolized by the analogy of assimilation, and since this term is in practice loosely used to designate harmonization by any means it will be well to examine this process first. On this basis, foreign immigrants coming to a receiving country are to be regarded as analogous to food particles taken into the body of a living organism. They are to be considered as the materials out of which the organism is to build up its future body. In order that this may take place, they must undergo a transformation into cells uniform in type with those which make up the body, and have always made it up from the beginning of its independent existence.

Just what does this mean in terms of nationality? It has already been shown that genuine immigrants — that is, those who come for permanent residence — inevitably become incorporated into the *population* of the receiving country. That is the racial aspect of the matter; it is a physical process involved in the very act of immigration. There is no way of preventing it. But we have seen that nationality is a very different thing from population. Nationality is a spiritual reality, existing in the realm of

THE MEANING OF ASSIMILATION

the sentiments, emotions, and intellect. The act of migration does not in any sense make the foreigner a member of the receiving nationality. In fact, no immigrant immediately after arrival is ever a member of the new nationality, any more than a morsel of food that has just passed the lips is at once a portion of the body. The foreign immigrant brings his nationality with him. He is still a member of the Greek nationality, or the Danish nationality, or whatever it may be, even though separated by thousands of miles from the bulk of those who compose that nationality.

The transformation that must take place, then, before the process of social assimilation is complete, must be a transformation in the elements or qualities of nationality. We have already seen what the most important of these are — language, religion, political ideas, moral standards, economic abilities, dress, recreation, food, ornamentation, family customs, all sorts of habits, traditions, beliefs, and loyalties. In all of these particulars the immigrant must be transformed into the type of the receiving nationality. He must react to social stimuli and respond to social situations in exactly the same way as if he had always lived in the midst of this nationality. Before assimilation is complete he must have lost all trace or suggestion of his foreign origin. A crisis in his native country must arouse no different sensations in his heart than in the case of any native of his new country. He must feel no sense of alienation with reference to his new compatriots, nor they any sense of distinction from him, because of his origin. He must rise to the appeals of loyalty and patriotism just as if he had never known a different nationality. He must have become completely one with the receiving body.

Defined in these terms, assimilation appears as a task of tremendous, almost insuperable, difficulty. In fact, it is doubtful whether, according to this conception, any adult immigrant to any country is ever completely assimilated. Generally speaking, the lower the age at which immigration takes place, the greater is the ease of assimilation, and therefore the greater the possibilities of its being accomplished. This is for two reasons. First, because the younger the immigrant is the less firmly has his original nationality been established, and so the easier it is to throw it off. Second, the younger the immigrant is the more plastic is his emotional nature and the more receptive to the impressions of the new environment. Complete assimilation may be possible if commenced at an early age and carried on under the most favorable circumstances.

To carry this analogy to its conclusion, it must be observed that in all this process the receiving nationality undergoes no alteration to correspond to the qualities of the foreign elements. There is one central standard, the existing national type, which is

THE MEANING OF ASSIMILATION

constantly preserved, and to which all the different types are made to conform. This does not mean at all the "standardizing of the immigrant" in the sense that is often claimed. It does not mean that all foreign-born members of the nationality must become individually exactly alike, any more than all the native-born are identical. Personal variety is not only unavoidable but wholly desirable. But it does mean that the differences which the foreign individual exhibits shall be those of personality, not the characteristic differences of a foreign nationality.

The second of the conceivable processes of national harmonization is symbolized by the melting pot. This, as has already been shown, involves the idea of mixture. It is an idea which applies with much accuracy to racial unification. The present question is: Does it apply to national unification? Can diverse nationalities be harmonized by mixing them together?

The nature of a mixture is that while each individual particle retains its original qualities unaltered the separate particles are so intimately associated and so evenly distributed that the general aspects of the whole mass appear as a uniform blending of the characteristics of the different kinds of components in the proportions in which those components exist. The crux of the whole question is whether the qualities of nationality are of such a sort that the human particles who embody them can be intimately mingled together, so that the various features of the group will be the composite representation of the qualities of the individuals.

This problem requires a further examination of the elements of nationality. Let us take up a few of the more important in turn. At the top stands language. Can languages be mixed? In one sense, possibly yes. It may be that under primitive conditions, when nationality is as yet amorphous, two or more different languages may be blended together into an entirely new language showing some of the characteristics of each of the components. Thus it is said that the modern Turkish language is built up out of three distinct sources. The English language itself obviously derives from several sources. But in the sense that the mixing of languages may be a device for group harmonization under modern conditions the answer is emphatically no! Well-established languages do not mix. They may borrow words, and perhaps some idioms, from each other, but each language remains distinctly itself. In many ancient cities diverse linguistic groups have lived in close association with each other for centuries without the formation of a composite medium of communication. In the city of Smyrna, for instance, the Turkish, Greek, and Armenian languages, not to mention innumerable minor tongues, have been spoken for many generations, yet there is no "Smyrna blend", nor is a knowledge of one of these languages as spoken

THE MEANING OF ASSIMILATION

in that city of the slightest use in conversing with a person who knows only one of the others. It would probably be impossible to find a single instance among the civilized countries of the world for hundreds of years past where group unity has been achieved by the fusing of languages.

Next comes religion. Here the principle applies with equal strength. The very nature of religion is exclusive and particularistic. It must be one thing or the other. It is true that religions are influenced by each other. Particularly when a group of people is converted from one religion to another they may carry over some of the forms and ritual of the old into the new. But the cleavage is none the less absolute between the two. In fact, a group of converts to a new religion is likely to be more intolerant toward the old belief than to some faith with which they have never been allied. Thus Mr. Wells observes: "Religious cults and priesthoods are sectarian by nature; they will convert, they will overcome, but they will never coalesce." [1]

Nowhere around us to-day do we see religions blending. In fact, the tendency seems to be all in the opposite direction. Certainly as far as the Christian religion is concerned the process has been a splitting up into innumerable minor sects, the distinctions between which often baffle any but the theologians, but which command such an uncom-

[1] H. G. Wells, "Outline of History", I: 242.

promising loyalty on the part of their adherents that all efforts toward consolidation are stubbornly and effectively resisted. A remarkable exception to this general rule is furnished by recent events in Canada. We are informed that the Presbyterian, Methodist, and Congregational churches in the Dominion have combined under the name of the United Church of Canada. This case, interesting as it is, is, however, merely a fusion of certain sects of a single religion, differing from each other only in minute nonessentials. As the newspaper account states, in very significant words, "The chief barriers to amalgamation proved to be sentimental rather than theological. Loyalties to honored names, honored forms, honored traditions, loomed large in the debates." [1] It is well to remember that this consolidation, probably unique in the history of religion, was accomplished in one of the most homogeneous nationalities in existence. Even so, not all the adherents of the old bodies could be persuaded to join the movement. Some remained outside, forming themselves into a "Presbyterian Association." Furthermore, from the point of view of social assimilation, the question may well be raised whether any such happy union would have been possible if each of the three sects had been associated with a distinct racial or national group. The United States Census Bureau in 1916 listed two hundred and two distinct religious denominations of sufficient

[1] New York *Times*, June 10, 1925.

THE MEANING OF ASSIMILATION

importance to be separately recorded. This was an increase of sixteen in ten years. Almost all of these are subdivisions of the Christian faith. Certainly, then, it is not to be expected that entirely different religions will blend.

The same is emphatically true of moral codes. The very nature of moral standards is that they are absolute. They cannot be mixed, combined, or blended. The almost inevitable effect of attempting to harmonize two diverse moral codes is to break down moral sanctions altogether. This is strikingly illustrated in the case of the second generation of immigrants in this country who appear to be, by all tests, the most nearly unmoral of any of the commonly recognized groups in the entire population. It is true that moral codes are constantly changing in every nationality, and that in an immigrant receiving country one of the factors of change may be the presence of foreign nationalities. But the process is in no sense analogous to mixture.

Another very important element in nationality is the family organization, and family customs and standards. Differences in this field are among the most serious obstacles to group coöperation, and harmonization is particularly difficult. It certainly can not be achieved by blending. The outlook of the Greek father who regards his ten-year-old son simply as a source of financial gain through the operation of the padrone system is too far removed from that of the typical American to leave any hope for adjustment through compromise. The Italian father who refused to let his daughter go to a hospital for a needed operation because she would have been forever dishonored by spending a night away from under his own roof saw no middle ground, and was only reconciled when a bed was provided for him in the same institution. Neither member of a Slavic couple engaged in the periodic exercise of wife-beating welcomes the intrusion of an outsider bent on mollifying the custom.

So we might go on down the long list of major and minor national traits. It might seem that in the case of some of the less vital factors such as dress, decoration, recreation, etc. there should be some possibility of combination. There is indeed a certain amount of borrowing, particularly in the matter of recreation. There are some games that are nearly universal, such as tops, marbles, and kites, and other sports find a limited acceptance in other than their native countries. Soccer, lacrosse, and cricket have made some headway in the United States, but are hardly as yet to be considered a part of the American nationality. On the upper levels of recreation — music, drama, and art — there is of course very free interchange. But this is ordinarily not in the least associated with population movements, and has little connection with the problems of national unification. It may seem strange that in some

THE MEANING OF ASSIMILATION 149

cases where there would be such a distinct gain from blending the process does not take place. Food customs furnish an excellent illustration. The dietary of the American people might be vastly enriched and improved by a judicious intermingling of foreign features. This does in fact take place among the cosmopolitan classes. But the dietary features of the American nationality itself have been very little altered by the immigration of thirty-five million foreigners from dozens of different nationalities. Professor Steiner, whose understanding of these matters is exceptional, comments upon the tenacity of food habits and predilections:

"American people wonder at the tenacity with which the immigrant clings to the foods of his Fatherland. It is not strange, for the nostrils, the lips, the whole body retain precious memories of odours and tastes which are seldom forgotten. I am inclined to believe that noodle soup, with the right kind of seasoning, touches more channels of memory than — say, a lullaby or even a picture of the homeland. The Jewish lawgivers knew this fact, although they never studied psychology, and every historic occurrence which they wished to memorialize is steeped in some dietary law and so forever preserved. They could trust the palate more than the spoken word or the written page." [1]

The simple fact is that, with negligible exceptions,

[1] E. A. Steiner, "From Alien to Citizen", page 68.

the traits of nationality will not combine, and so nationalities as a whole can not be mixed. The reason is not difficult to comprehend. National traits are mass realities, existing in groups, not in individuals. We speak of the nationality of an individual. It is more accurate to speak of an individual as belonging to a nationality than as having a nationality. In the case of a mixture a single particle can slip into the mixture and become a part of it, keeping its own character and affecting the nature of the mixture by just so much. But in the case of a nationality the foreign particle does not become a part of the nationality until he has become assimilated to it. Previous to that time he is an extraneous factor, like undigested, and possibly indigestible, matter in the body of a living organism. That being the case, the only way he can alter the nationality is by injuring it, by impeding its functions. He can not produce a normal, healthy modification in his own direction.

It follows, then, that the attempt to mix nationalities must result not in a new type of composite nationality but in the destruction of all nationality. No one of the components can survive the process if it is carried too far.

This is the outstanding fallacy of the melting pot. It applies a figure that is appropriate only in the racial sense to a problem that is preponderantly national. It represents unification in terms of a process which,

THE MEANING OF ASSIMILATION 151

for the greater part of the task of unification, will not work.

If the truth were otherwise in this matter the history of the Balkans would have been very different from what it has been. The Balkan populations are often referred to as a racial conglomeration, and to a considerable extent the designation is accurate. But the heart of the Balkan tangle is not racial, but national. The inhabitants of this unfortunate area are broken up into incompatible groups not by racial differentiations — most of which they would be quite unable to detect — but by languages, religions, customs, social habits, and, perhaps most of all, by traditional group loyalties, the origin of which few would be able to trace and the nature of which few would be able to explain. In fact, the history and present situation of the Balkans suggests as the ultimate truth the conclusion that the contact of diverse nationalities, far from tending to produce a coalescing, actually tends to accentuate the differences and to intensify the unreasoning tenacity with which each group clings to its own particular traits.

When, as a result of the revelations of the War, it became clear that the figure of the melting pot was an anomaly, an attempt was made to develop a third conception of the process of national harmonization which had been envisaged by a few observers for some time previously. As a symbol of this idea the figure of a "weaving machine" was suggested:

"We have heard much, in the past, of the great American 'Melting Pot.' Why not think, instead, of a great American 'Weaving Machine'? Which kind of an America do you prefer: an America whose many national strains have been so merged into a common mass as to resemble nothing so much as the colorless drab which results from mixing many colors, or an America which resembles, rather, a brilliant fabric into which these national strains have been so woven that, like colors, none have been destroyed but all preserved in their original hues and so harmonized that each has gained lustre by the new association and contrast? Do you want a living and a growing America?"

The figure of the weaving machine never achieved much popularity. Probably few readers of this page ever heard of it. Undoubtedly this was due in part to the fact that it lacked the intangible qualities of an appealing symbol. It was artificial and labored, not picturesque. But another reason must have been its utter absurdity when subjected to a critical examination and analysis. At first blush it may seem like both a broad-minded and a constructive program that the traits of all the nations of Europe — only the best traits, we may assume; the others, by some undescribed social necromancy, having been sloughed off — should be woven together into a uniquely rich national pattern. But the moment one stops to consider exactly what is involved in such a program the

THE MEANING OF ASSIMILATION 153

futility of it becomes obvious enough. What kind of a nation would the United States be if we were to succeed in "weaving" in among our own traits the languages of Poland, Turkey, and Portugal, the family institutions of Bulgaria, Italy, and Sweden, the political ideas of England, Russia, and Greece, the sanitary customs of Roumania, Switzerland, and France, the economic systems of Albania, Spain, and Belgium, the moral codes of the Balkan States and Scandinavia, and so on *ad infinitum?* The very essence of nationality is uniformity throughout the entire body in important particulars. And in just what way are the strands of different nationalities to be represented? By individuals? By local groups? By organizations affiliated on a national scale?

The absurdity of this whole conception becomes especially clear when it is recalled how large a part of nationality consists in loyalties. To what is the individual to be loyal in this national coat-of-many-colors? How much loyalty of any sort would survive such a process? Yet the idea seems to be very alluring to certain types of mind. Thus Doctor Eliot is quoted as having said recently, "What we want in this country is a number of races with various gifts, each contributng its own peculiar qualities to the common welfare. . . . The Irish have never been assimilated in America anywhere and it is not desirable that they should be." The Jews "should keep their race individuality in America just as the Irish have done." Horace M. Kallen has devoted a volume to the support of the same general proposition.[1]

Reviewing these three proposed methods of unification, it becomes clear that the only one which can survive a close comparison with the facts of nationality is that symbolized by the metabolic analogy of assimilation. If this interpretation is accepted, it must be confessed that the implications with reference to the stranger in our midst are rigid and harsh enough. It is he who must undergo the entire transformation; the true member of the American nationality is not called upon to change in the least. The traits of foreign nationality which the immigrant brings with him are not to be mixed or interwoven. They are to be *abandoned*. The standard to which he must conform has been already fixed by forces quite outside himself, quite outside any individual, native or foreign, fixed by all the factors, topographical, climatic, racial, historical, fortuitous, which have worked together to make the American nationality what it is. A harsh situation, indeed! but a situation the harshness of which is determined not by the inclination or wish of any person or group of persons, but by the inherent qualities of human nature and social organization. It can therefore not be eliminated by any sentimental aspiration, however gen-

[1] "Culture and Democracy in the United States."

erous or altruistic. If immigration is to continue, and if our nation is to be preserved, we must all, natives and foreigners alike, resign ourselves to the inevitable truth that unity can be maintained only through the complete sacrifice of extraneous national traits on the part of our foreign elements. There is no "give-and-take" in assimilation.

CHAPTER VIII

AMERICANIZATION

THE customary use of the melting-pot figure in pre-War days was fallacious not only with respect to the process of social unification but also with respect to the fact of unification. It implied not only that the United States was a melting pot but that it was melting. It assumed that "E Pluribus Unum" could be accepted as a literal interpretation of the immigration problem.

This view was doubtless shared by the great majority of the American people. It is true that in the two or three decades just before the War the evidences of nonassimilation grew rather intrusive and insistent. The congested, specialized "colonies" of foreign peoples, not only in our great cities, but also in many rural districts, were too numerous and too conspicuous to be ignored. Everybody talked familiarly about "Ghettos", "Little Italys", and "Little Hungarys", but it was easy to convince one's self that these were merely transitional features, and that while the "colony" itself might be permanent the population of the colony was a constantly shifting one. The foreign settlement was looked upon simply as a way station on the route to unification. Comfort was drawn from the assumed complete assimilation of the earlier immigrant groups, Irish, German, and Scandinavian, ignoring of course the fact, now so clearly recognized, that not all foreign groups are equally assimilable, as well as the probability, not so plainly recognized, that even these earlier groups were not so completely assimilated as appearances indicated. The idea that the melting pot would not work automatically, or that it needed some deliberate tending, found little lodgment in the popular mind.

Yet even before the War the evidences of the failure of assimilation were plain enough to those who had the will and the insight to read them. The German "Turnverein", the Bohemian "Sokol", the Greek "Community", and a thousand-and-one other foreign-American societies were to be found on every hand. The term "hyphenated American" was already popular. The Irish vote, the Swedish vote, and various other foreign votes were well enough recognized by the politicians at least. Events of a more or less spectacular nature occurring from time to time were sufficient to give the warning. A single typical instance will suffice as an illustration.

In December, 1911, a meeting was held in Carnegie Hall, New York City, for the purpose of endorsing the treaties of arbitration with Great Britain and France which were in process of negotiation. This meeting was violently interrupted and virtually broken up by a group of persons of foreign ancestry, though not all of foreign birth, on the ground that the ratification of these treaties would be an affront against Germany. Two months later some of these same persons were instrumental in organizing a society the purpose of which was to defeat the plan to celebrate the completion of one hundred years of peace between this country and Great Britain. The significant feature is that these agitators were officials or members of certain avowed German-American and Irish-American societies, and the animus of their objections was a traditional antipathy to England. Doubtless there were many genuine Americans who, for various reasons, were opposed to both of these proposals. Americans always differ on practically all important questions. But when an organized group of persons, or even a single individual, opposes a measure for reasons traceable directly to origin in and affiliation with some foreign country, that is sure proof of nonassimilation.

But the very familiarity of such evidences dulled their significance, and their total weight was easily offset in most minds by a catchy figure of speech.

The suddenness with which the War revealed the true situation was spectacular. The explanation of this remarkable effect is probably to be found in the fact, already frequently mentioned, that nationality is largely a matter of loyalty, and that the display of loyalty in times of stress is one of the surest tests of nationality. The outstanding distinction between peace time and war time is found in the varying demands upon loyalty and occasions for displaying it. A divided allegiance, or a wholly un-American allegiance, which might drift along unnoticed for years in times of quietude, is thrown into sharp relief by the psychology of war. This phenomenon, at the time of the Great War, was of course most conspicuous in the case of our German population, and those portions of our Austro-Hungarian population whose associations with the Dual Empire had been such as to throw their allegiance on the side of the Central Powers. Many persons of German birth or parentage who had been accepted in their communities as ordinary members of American society found, possibly sometimes to their own surprise, that their fundamental loyalty was still to the mother country, and in some instances revealed the fact by their conduct. Pitiable in the extreme was the case of those whose major devotion and volitional allegiance were to the United States but who could not banish a deep-seated affection and sympathy for the country of their origin.

But while the alien spirit of our foreign population was most evident in the case of those groups which were affiliated with our enemies, it was none the less real and active among those whose native States Fate had decreed should be among our Allies. It was easy during these critical times to get the impression that some of the newer immigrant peoples were more fully assimilated, more truly American, than the Germans and Austrians, simply because they were at one with us on the great issues of the War. But if the situation had been such that Germany was lined up with the United States against an array of powers including Italy and Greece (as is easily conceivable in the case of the "next war") it would have been emphatically demonstrated that the ties of foreign nationality were just as strong among the new immigration as among the old. Those who dealt at first hand with the conglomeration of nationalities that made up the American army had abundant evidence of the alien character of a considerable proportion of the raw recruits.

Just as the importance of national unity was intensified by the War, so the national heterogeneity of our population was increasingly emphasized. There was a certain grim humor in the speed with which many of those who had previously been the most ardent champions of the doctrine of the melting pot hastened to recognize the undeniable, and loudly to proclaim the failure of assimilation up to date. Thus Miss Frances Kellor in her book, "Straight America": "We now know also that we are not in a position to participate disinterestedly and courageously in the international adjustments that will take place at the close of the war. . . . We but dimly realize that a united, not a divided nation must enter

AMERICANIZATION

the lists. . . . We see a conglomeration of colonies and ghettos and immigrant sections in our large cities, and the country dotted with settlements quite as un-American as anything to be found abroad. We face the fact that America is not first in the hearts of every resident, that not every man works for America, and that not every man trusts her present or believes in her future. This is still the land of promise for the 'bird of passage' who exploits us, and whom we pluck in return. Thanks to the war, we have been freed from the delusion that we are a united nation marching steadily along an American highway of peace, prosperity, common ideals, beliefs, language, and purpose. Security and prosperity have blinded us to the fact that we do not all speak the same language nor follow the same flag." [1]

In the same vein Miss Grace Abbott declares, "It is none the less true that unity of religion, unity of race, unity of ideals do not exist in the United States. We are many nationalities scattered across a continent." [2] It is not surprising, perhaps, that in making this sudden shift, these authors should have swung to the opposite extreme, ignoring the vast, stable sub-stratum of unity represented by probably five sixths of the population composed of native-born and truly assimilated foreigners.

This new realization and acceptance of the facts of nonassimilation was naturally followed by a deter-

[1] Pages 3, 4, 5. [2] "The Immigrant and the Community", page 277.

mination to do something about it. It was natural also that one of the chief moves in carrying out this determination was to fall back on the favorite American expedient and appoint committees. Finally, it was both natural and inevitable that one of the main features of the new program should be the selection of a winning slogan or catchword. The slogan chosen was "Americanization", and there followed immediately one of the most vivid illustrations of the potency of the symbol to be found in our entire history.

The word "Americanization" was not itself new. It would probably be difficult to discover just when and by whom it was first coined, but it was in common use years before the War. What gave it its significance after the War was its promotion into a symbol for a new idea or set of ideas. As is the case with every symbol, the idea it represented was but dimly comprehended by the great majority of those who eagerly hailed the symbol. In fact, of course, it was the idea that was important, not the catchword.

Doubtless there was a wide difference in the minds of many persons as to the exact ideas represented by the "Americanization Movement" in the early days of that remarkable phenomenon. But one central principle stood out quite clearly and still remains the distinguishing feature of "Americanization." Briefly stated, it was the recognition of the fact that assimilation had not been achieved, and therefore presumably could not be achieved, by the spontaneous play of natural social forces, and the determination to bring it to pass by deliberate, artificial methods. It was the erection of assimilation into a "problem", and the determination to find and apply a solution for that problem. It was the organization of deliberate, purposeful effort to promote national unification.

It would not be profitable in this connection to inquire into the origin and affiliations of the chief original Americanization committees. Few individuals took occasion to inquire at the time. The important fact was, and is, that there were committees. This meant organization, centralization, direction, efficiency. Some of the committees, at least, gave evidence of an ample supply of funds and displayed many impressive names on their letterheads. Why inquire as to who appointed the committees or where their funds came from? As was to be expected, the first result of this situation was a marked subsidence of the wave of consternation and alarm about the immigration situation which had been raised by the revelations of the War. People said to themselves, in effect, "It's all right now. There is a committee at work on this problem and we can put our minds at ease. Everything will be taken care of."

We all recall very vividly, however, that the enterprise of deliberate and positive Americanization was by no means confined to the original committees, or to any committees. The Movement became a popular crusade. It caught the public fancy, harmonizing as it did with the intensified patriotism and the eager desire to render social service which characterized the period. Tens of thousands of persons from all walks of life threw themselves into the undertaking.

It was perhaps in keeping with the interest and faith in education, which has been called the outstanding feature of the American nationality, that the task of Americanization should have presented itself to the pioneers in the movement primarily as an educational matter. Recognizing that the process of assimilation consists in the elimination of unlikeness, it was natural that in considering the unlikeness of the foreigner they should have been impressed with the difference in what he knew. It was perfectly clear that one of the great barriers that separated the native from the foreigner was the fact that the native knew certain things that the foreigner did not know. Prominent among these were the English language and United States civics and history. The first and most obvious step in Americanization, therefore, seemed to be to teach these things to the foreigner.

Thereupon there was launched upon the country one of the most remarkable campaigns of intensive specialized education that the world has ever known. Every conceivable educational device was utilized.

The land was flooded with lessons, lectures, and literature. Night schools and shop classes were organized. Rallies, pageants, and conferences were held. A special magazine was established and issued for a few numbers. An elaborate training course for workers among immigrants was planned and offered for adoption among colleges and universities. As the movement grew, and the needs of the immigrant woman as well as the immigrant man were recognized, classes were set up in millinery, dressmaking, diet, and the American care of babies. To these enterprises time, money, and personal service were contributed by men and women, professionals and volunteers, with a devotion and enthusiasm which could be enlisted only by loyalty to the nation in a time of stress and danger. Coming at any other time, when we were not accustomed to displays of self-sacrifice and public spirit, the Americanization Movement would have been a striking exhibition of the operation of altruistic sentiments.

How remarkable, then, that in the course of two or three years the movement should have burned itself out almost completely! Night schools diminished. Special classes were abandoned. Newspaper notices and public propaganda disappeared. Committees vanished into thin air. One after another the secondary features were discontinued until Americanization came very nearly to approximate the popular conception of it, — "Teaching English to foreigners." Enthusiasm waned and sentiment changed until the very word "Americanization" became discredited, and even those who were still actually engaged in the work shunned the title. The whole situation was epitomized by a certain teacher who for weeks had been preparing her pupils for that elaborate exhibition presented in one of the armories of New York City and called, "America's Making." Coming into a schoolroom where were several of her fellow teachers, after the last performance had been given, she dropped wearily into a chair and exclaimed, "Thank Heaven! America's made."

The failure of the early phase of the Americanization Movement was due to one fundamental cause, which expressed itself in a variety of aspects. This was an almost complete lack of understanding of the nature of assimilation on the part of those who engineered the movement, and of course an even greater deficiency among the rank and file of the workers. The most obvious evidence of this lack was the confusion of a means with an end. It was the assumption that the difference between a member of the American nationality and one of some foreign nationality was essentially a matter of knowledge, and that therefore it could be corrected by education. If the discussion of nationality in the foregoing pages has in any measure fulfilled its purpose it should be perfectly clear that the true test of nationality is not what you know but how you feel. It is perfectly true that before you can feel certain sentiments toward a nation you must know something about it. But the knowledge and the feeling are not identical, nor does the feeling necessarily follow the knowledge. The knowledge, if it has any efficiency at all, is merely the means whereby the feeling is achieved. The feeling is the final end.

The fallacy of identifying information with national allegiance should have been made perfectly clear by the events of the War itself. The clash of interest between the United States and Germany threw into bold relief the fact that there were many Germans in this country, not only foreign-born persons, but also their descendants of the second and third generation, who knew English perfectly, who had a better grasp of American civics and history than many members of the old native stock, who dressed, ate, and cared for their babies in characteristic American style, whose ultimate allegiance nevertheless was with the "Vaterland" and not with the land of their residence. Education, information, and knowledge had been powerless to sever them from their natural loyalty to the country of their origin. As already observed, the same situation would have been equally notable in the case of other foreign nationalities had they been ranged against us in the great conflict.

In fact, if knowledge were assimilation, it would be possible to Americanize foreigners by means of educational activities carried on in their native lands. In many ways, the educational processes themselves might be more effective there than here. We could send corps of special teachers over to Italy, Greece, or Poland, and after a few months of intensive training ship ready-made Americans over to the United States who would need no further assimilation. The palpable absurdity of this assumption shows how unsound is the identification of knowledge with Americanization.

Americanization is not an educational process, though the Americanization Movement was, and is, essentially an educational program. True Americanization is a spiritual and emotional transformation. Shall we say, then, that the entire effort that went into the early Americanization activities was sheer loss, and that those who are still carrying on Americanization work in its simpler and standardized form are wasting their time? By no means! To point out the fallacy of confusing means with ends does not at all imply that the means are useless. We must assuredly have the means in order to achieve the ends. The mistake of the early Americanizers was in not seeing or going far enough, in assuming that they could stop with the means.

All gratitude is due for the results that have already been accomplished in training a certain proportion of our foreign population in certain features of the American nationality. All support and encourage-

AMERICANIZATION

ment should be accorded to those who are carrying on the enterprise. Their work is absolutely indispensable. Without some knowledge of the American nationality assimilation into it is wholly impossible. This is particularly true of the English language. Since nationality is largely a matter of ideas, there can be no assimilation without an interchange of ideas, and there can be no traffic in ideas without a common means of communication. An easy use of the English language is a *sine qua non* for assimilation into the United States, and a knowledge of civics and history is most useful. But all these are not enough. They are the channels, the gateways, the instruments of assimilation, but they are not assimilation. What more is needed, and how it may be supplied, will be considered in a later connection.

A second great result of the failure of the early Americanizers to grasp the real nature of assimilation was their inability to put themselves in the place of the immigrant, and to understand the psychological conditions of Americanization. One expression of this lack of comprehension was the common assumption that assimilation is a voluntary process, that it can be accomplished by an act of the will. As a result of this assumption the alien was quite generally *blamed* for his nonassimilation. He was treated as if his failure to Americanize was his own fault, and it was proposed to penalize him for it in various ways. The act of assimilation was conceived of much like the act of conversion in an old-fashioned revival. It was assumed that if sufficient pressure could be brought to bear upon the immigrant, and he could be worked up into a certain emotional state, he could deliberately "take the stand" and thereupon go forth forever after an American.

One embodiment of this idea is found in that remarkable compilation known as "The American's Creed" which is widely used in our public school system and is regarded as an important part of the one hundred per cent. American influence of that institution. It reads as follows:

"I believe in the United States of America as a government of the people, by the people, for the people; whose just powers are derived from the consent of the governed; a democracy in a republic; a sovereign nation of many sovereign states; a perfect union, one and inseparable; established upon those principles of freedom, equality, justice, and humanity for which American patriots sacrificed their lives and fortunes.

"I therefore believe it is my duty to my country to love it; to support its constitution; to obey its laws; to respect its flag; and to defend it against all enemies."

Now, however much we may admire the majority of the lofty sentiments thus gathered together, what shall we say of the assertion, "It is my duty to my country to love it"? Was ever a case known where a person loved a thing because he was told that was his duty? What have love and duty to do with each other? It is to be feared that human nature is just contrary enough so that the surest way to make the average mortal hate an object is to tell him repetitiously that he ought to love it.

CHAPTER IX

ENFORCED PATRIOTISM

ONE result of this incomprehension of the immigrant's psychology is the notion, shared by the majority of Americans, that in the case of the foreigner in the United States a certain revolutionary transformation not only may be expected to take place, but ought to take place, which we do not expect to occur in the case of the American in a foreign land, and which arouses our scorn and condemnation if it does occur. We expect all foreigners to be assimilated in the United States and blame them if they are not; we do not expect any American to be assimilated in a foreign land, and blame him if he is. This antithesis may be emphasized by putting it in personal terms.

Suppose that you, John Smith, native American of old New England stock, graduating from college at the age of twenty-two, had received an attractive offer of a business position in Germany. You accepted the opening, and went to Germany, taking your young wife with you. In order to make the most of your opportunities you threw yourself unreservedly into the German life. You soon became fluent in the language, you took every occasion to familiarize yourself with the German outlook on

ENFORCED PATRIOTISM

life, and participated as fully as possible in every phase of the German nationality. You attended German opera, read German books, took part in religious services in German churches, spent your evenings in German beer gardens, and by every means got as near to the heart of the German people as possible. Your children, born in Germany, went to German schools, played with German children, spoke German more readily than English, were never taken to visit the United States. So things went on until in the year 1917 you finished your fiftieth year of life. Would the declaration of hostilities between the United States and Germany have found you a German? Would you have thrown all your resources and influence into the German cause? Would you have urged your sons to enlist in the German army, and would they have been not only willing to obey you, but fired with a zeal for the land of their birth? Or would you not instead have closed up your affairs as hastily as possible, packed up your belongings, and taken the first boat for America? Would you not have expected even your children to feel the deep thrill of allegiance to the homeland of their ancestors, and, however painful the act of turning their backs upon friends and associations, to respond unreservedly to the ultimate appeal of nationality?

Why should we so readily expect the foreigner to be assimilated in the United States when we do not expect the American to be assimilated in a foreign land? "For the very simple reason", the genuine American will reply, "that America *is* the best and finest country in the world." And he will be quite correct. America is the best country in the world — for Americans. We are under not the slightest obligation to concede or alter one jot or one tittle of the American nationality to suit the wishes or inclinations of those who come from abroad to live among us. We are wholly justified in demanding assimilation at the quickest possible rate as a condition for permitting any considerable number of them to come. But this does not mean that we should charge tardy assimilation up against the individual immigrant, or attempt to penalize any foreigner whom we have taken the responsibility of admitting for his failure to become assimilated in any specified time. He, too, has grown up thinking that his native country is the finest country in the world, and he loves it just as naturally as the American loves the United States. The conditions of assimilation lie largely beyond the voluntary control of the immigrant, and as far as they are subject to the human will the responsibility for creating them lies, as we shall see, fully as much with the native American as with the foreigner. It is equally cruel and senseless to attempt to cajole or bully the alien into Americanization. The very fact that he has taken the initial step of coming to the United States indicates that he regards

ENFORCED PATRIOTISM 175

some, at least, of the features of the American nationality as preferable to his own. One would like to go further and say that the fact of migration indicates also the "will to assimilate." One would like to believe that every immigrant comes to this country inspired with admiration for the American nationality as a whole, and animated by a desire to become absorbed in that nationality as soon as possible. Unfortunately, the truth is that the feature of the American nationality which operates as the chief drawing card in the great majority of cases among the recent immigrants is the opportunity to make money. The economic motive is recognized by all students as the outstanding force back of immigration in the case of most individuals of most foreign groups. In earlier days other features of our nationality, related to political, social, and religious freedom and opportunity, doubtless played a large part. But as democracy and opportunity have become more widespread in Europe and (it must be confessed) less characteristic of America the advantages of the United States in these particulars have become much less effective in stimulating migration. The curve of immigration in the last fifty years has followed very closely the curve of economic prosperity in the United States. So it will not do to assume an ardent desire to assimilate on the part of every immigrant. But neither may it be assumed that this desire can be created on the part of those who do not possess it, or made more effective on the part of those who do possess it, by preaching at them, threatening them, or prating to them about duty.

This misunderstanding of the psychology of the immigrant was matched, and in part produced, by a false mental attitude on the part of the Americanizers toward the foreigners. There was a Pharisaical, holier-than-thou approach very conspicuous in the early activities. It has not altogether disappeared, alas! even yet. Very prominent leaders in very respectable and well-intentioned Americanization agencies may still be heard referring to the immigrants as "these people." There was a prevailing attitude of standing above the level of the foreigner and reaching down a kindly hand to pull him up to a higher station. Americanization work was a sort of glorified slumming. It was the "Lady Bountiful" relationship brought up to date and transferred to the political field. All of which is reprehensible not merely because it is silly and snobbish, but because it so completely confuses the issue and obscures the legitimate grounds upon which America bases her requirements of the immigrant. The United States demands assimilation of the immigrant not because he is less wise, or less intelligent, or less good than the American, or inferior in any respect, but because he is different. The United States says to the immigrant, "We have our own ways and you have your ways. Your ways are not our ways. We prefer our ways just because they are our own, and because our whole national life is built upon and around them. It is naturally very hard for you to give up your own ways, even though you want to. But we can not tolerate the danger of having too many persons in our midst whose ways are different from ours. So if you wish to remain among us we hope that you will utilize every opportunity to learn and adopt our ways, and on our part we stand ready to help you by every means at our command."

The condescending attitude referred to produced rather bizarre results at times. It led to the use of blanket methods, many of which assumed that all foreigners belonged necessarily to the wage-earning class. Form letters were sent out to the wives of aliens who had taken out their first papers, urging them to slip citizenship leaflets into their husbands' dinner pails, and not to wear shawls but hats when they accompanied their husbands to night school, regardless of the fact that the recipient might be a person at least the equal in refinement and *savoir faire* of the person who composed the letter.

A third indictment against the early Americanization movement may be found in its habitual emphasis upon the motive of narrow self-interest as a stimulus to Americanization. The foreigner was continually urged to become assimilated because of what he could get out of it. There was a ceaseless reiteration of certain advantages, mostly of a distinctly material sort, which the alien might expect to receive as a reward for taking out his citizenship papers. This feature is excellently illustrated by the "Pay Envelope Series" which was issued in accordance with the wholesale methods mentioned in the foregoing paragraph. Some of the injunctions emphasized in these little leaflets were:

YOUR DUTY

It is your duty to support your family.
It is your duty to save your money.
It is your duty to become a
GOOD AMERICAN CITIZEN

BECOME AN AMERICAN

Make Application for Citizenship
Prepare for the Examination
Join a Citizenship Class

AMERICAN CITIZENSHIP MEANS

Better Work
Better Home
Better Chance for your Children
Better Opportunities

You Can Have These by Becoming an American Citizen

BETTER AMERICA

Better Home   Better Work
Citizenship Gives You These

MONEY

Save your money.
You work for your money.
Let your money work for you.
Deposit it in a Savings Bank and receive interest.
Something saved to-day will provide for to-morrow.

There was also an Americanization poster, printed in many languages and embellished with a border of red, white, and blue. Its message was:

AMERICA FIRST

Learn English. Attend Night School. Become a Citizen.
It means a better opportunity
and a better home in America.
It means a better job.
It means a better chance for your children.
It means a better America.

In the center is a pictorial representation of Uncle Sam extending the right hand of fellowship to a sturdy, clean-cut foreigner dressed in overalls and bearing the inevitable pick. With his left hand Uncle Sam points invitingly to a naturalization judge who is smilingly delivering citizenship papers to a newly made member of the American nation. In the background appear on one side a public school building, and on the other a notably attractive and commodious country residence, in front of which a charming wife and daughter have come out to greet the well-dressed, alert *pater familias* — obviously intended to represent the perfect flower of the two processes just described.

It would probably be difficult to find a more flagrantly immoral set of doctrines propagated in the name of patriotism and humanity than those typified by the instances just given. They are immoral in the first place because they are profoundly untrue. There is no basis for the assertion that citizenship gives the foreigner a better job, a better home, and a better chance for his children. Perhaps on the average, and in the long run, citizenship may have an infinitesimal influence in that direction. There are, to be sure, some jobs of a semi-official character which in some communities are open only to citizens, and they may be exceptionally good jobs in the sense that they bring a large return relative to the amount of effort expended. But they do not seriously affect the whole labor situation. And the immigrant is not concerned with long-time averages. If an alien is told that he may have better work, a better home, and better opportunities by becoming a citizen, and if he believes it, he will expect personally, within a reasonably short time after naturalization, to find himself in the actual enjoyment of these blessings. If instead, as is much more likely to be the case, he finds himself unemployed, without prospects, and forced to move from his three-room tenement into one foul room in the basement, he will rightfully conclude that he has been duped, he will wrongly hold the government to blame, and the first long step will have been taken in the making of a Red Radical.

The second basis of immorality in this propaganda is found in the character of its appeal. Even if it were true that the foreigner could improve his economic situation by becoming a citizen, it is a very peculiar conception of patriotism and national loyalty that would rely upon this motive as the only one adequate to stir the alien to seek assimilation. It portrays the American nationality as a thing of so little value in itself that there is no reason for desiring it except for the material advantages it brings, instead of presenting it as an object of so great intrinsic worth that much material well-being might profitably be sacrificed to attain it. It tends to develop in the immigrant's mind exclusively the idea of what he can get out of America instead of cultivating a recognition of what he owes to America, and a sense of obligation to do what he can for America.

The insistent urging of the alien to become a citizen which is so marked in the foregoing quotations was one of the most insidious and pernicious phases of the original Americanization Movement. The notions back of it have not entirely disappeared even yet. They rest upon one of the most remarkable cases of inverted logic that could be found in the whole political history of the nation. The process of reasoning (if such it may be called) which led to the conclusion that the alien should be urged to become a citizen may be summarized somewhat in this wise: "Every foreigner who has been in this country a sufficient length of time, and who has developed the right attitude toward this country, will wish to become a citizen. There are millions of foreigners who have not become citizens, and who therefore presumably have not the right attitude toward this country. Therefore let us make them all citizens." In other words, it was a striking case of the illusion of the label. As observed in the early pages of this book, we are necessarily so dependent upon labels that we pathetically desire to believe that a thing is what its label says it is. It is just one step — an easy step, if not a logical one — to delude ourselves into believing that if a thing is not what we wish it to be, the difficulty can be removed if only some one will paste the right label across it. This illusion is fostered by the fact that few of us, habitually, are responsible for the labeling. But we have a naïve confidence in the labelers, and shun the notion that the label can be applied unless the quality is there. So on with the label!

This seems to have been exactly the train of thought back of the campaign for enforced or coerced citizenship. We were acutely aware of the menace of large masses of unassimilated foreigners. We assumed that the naturalization paper was the label of assimilation. So we proceeded to urge the alien to become naturalized. If any justification whatever is to be found for this process, it must be looked for in a vague but effective confidence in our naturalization procedure, which assumed that no alien could become a citizen who was not in fact pretty well assimilated. If this assumption were true, there would be much less fault to find with the public attitude in question. If it were true that the requirements of our naturalization law and the methods of the examining judges were such as to provide a reliable test of the alien's actual fitness for citizenship and if no alien could get citizenship who did not measure up to these tests, then, however illogical the method, there would be little harm in urging foreigners to become citizens. To urge them to become citizens would be equivalent to urging them to become assimilated, though even so the emphasis would be decidedly wrong.

Unfortunately, however, this assumption is very far from the truth. The tests imposed upon the alien by our naturalization law afford no evidence whatever as to his actual assimilation, and impose no barrier to the naturalization of a completely unassimilated foreigner, nor are the judges able, by tests of their own devising, to assure themselves that the alien is already a true American in spirit. Statements as sweeping as these evidently call for confirmation. This confirmation is to be found in an examination of the naturalization law itself.

The essential requirements for naturalization in the United States were enacted into law about a century and a quarter ago, and have been but little modified since. In an indefinite and implicit way they assume that some degree, at least, of assimilation should precede naturalization, and they set up certain tests of this assimilation. In these tests reliance is placed on two kinds of evidence, first, facts that, theoretically at least, can be established on a positive basis, and second, a mental attitude on the part of the alien which is expressed by his own statements and is practically incapable of verification. Let us examine these two categories in turn. The candidate must be a free white person, or an "alien of African nativity" or a "person of African descent." These last two classes were added after the Civil War to harmonize our naturalization standards with the enfranchisement of the negroes. The candidate must be twenty-one years of age, and must have resided continuously five years in the United States, and one year in the State in which he makes application. At least two years, and not more than seven years, before he applies for citizenship he must have declared his intention of doing so and have received his "first paper." He must be able to speak English (unless registered under the Homestead Laws) and must be able to sign his name. As to these requirements, there is no serious difficulty in securing a reasonable certainty as to the facts. Certain other of the fac-

ENFORCED PATRIOTISM

tual requirements are not capable of documentary support. These are that the candidate must be of good moral character, attached to the principles of the Constitution of the United States, and not an anarchist or a polygamist. To support his claims in these respects the candidate must have two witnesses, themselves citizens of the United States, who must testify particularly as to his residence in the United States, his good moral character, his attachment to the Constitution, and his general fitness for citizenship. By omission, the law seems to imply that the witnesses can hardly be expected to take the responsibility as to the candidate's anarchistic or polygamous predilections. These, then, are the facts upon which the judge is supposed to be reasonably assured before he issues the naturalization paper.

In the second category, the tests of the candidate's state of mind, the law specifies that he must renounce any hereditary title or order of nobility (once this is done, of course, it becomes a fact) and all allegiance and fidelity to any foreign potentate, prince, city, or State of which he is a subject. He must affirm his intention to reside permanently in the United States, and must declare on oath that he will "support and defend the Constitution and laws of the United States against all enemies, foreign and domestic, and bear true faith and allegiance to the same." This last provision is obviously essentially the same as the "attachment to the Constitution", included in the first category, and which really belongs in the second, as it is something about which only the alien himself can have positive assurance.

Examining these requirements in detail, it appears that the first provision represents a determination on the part of the lawmakers that this is to be essentially a white man's country. The inclusion of Africans is clearly an illogical and unpremeditated exception, necessitated by an early, fundamental, and irremediable error in economic and social policy. This provision sets up the racial requirement for citizenship, and is exceedingly important, but it has no direct connection with assimilation, for if a foreigner is not qualified to meet it by birth, no amount of assimilation can fit him for it. Consequently, the exhortations to become a citizen can have application only to those who, quite independently, of their own volition, are already prepared to meet this particular test. The requirement of age is an obvious one, and is also one which no amount of urging can affect in the least. There remain, then, the questions of residence, of anarchism, polygamy, the ability to speak English and sign one's name, of good moral character, and of attachment to the Constitution. Of these, good moral character is either meaningless or an axiomatic commonplace, having nothing to do with assimilation. The requirements about anarchism, polygamy, the English language, and signing one's name, are a recognition of certain outstanding features of the American nationality, very good as far as they go. They are, in truth, practically the only factual tests of assimilation in the whole naturalization law. This leaves attachment to the Constitution, which, as already observed, really belongs in the second category, and the five-year residence requirement.

There can be no doubt that, in so far as the necessity of establishing factual tests of assimilation was recognized by the framers of this law, chief reliance was placed upon the period of residence. It still remains the only really significant tangible test in the category of facts, except for some obvious and indisputable preliminaries. And the tragic weakness of our whole naturalization procedure is glaringly revealed when it is realized, as it must be upon a moment's consideration, that under modern conditions this test has literally no conclusive significance at all. When this provision was written into the law in the early decades of the American nation, it was assumed that no foreigner could live in the United States for a continuous period of five years without being incorporated into the essential activities of the American nationality and catching the spirit of American institutions. It was assumed that after five years of such contact the alien could hardly help being favorably inclined toward this nation, and that the only evidence of his loyalty to the country that was really required was his own statement to that effect. At the time when the law was framed there were excellent grounds for these assumptions. The United States was a new, sparsely settled country, with simple and almost primitive social institutions. Life was organized on an intimate and personal basis. Acquaintanceship among the members of the small communities was spontaneous and inclusive. The immigrants themselves were mostly persons from nationalities closely affiliated in spirit with the American. They spoke the English language, or closely related languages. Their fundamental outlook on life harmonized easily with that of the Americans. Most of them had faced great hardships, dangers, and sacrifices to come to this country, and were attracted by its political, religious, and social features as well as by its economic advantages. Under such conditions it transpired, almost inevitably, that any foreigner who lived for five years in this new land did make the acquaintance of a number of Americans, did mingle with them in a wide variety of activities, did share with them the interchange of ideas and emotions that produces unification, and did undergo a genuine spiritual transformation. He could hardly avoid assimilating influences even if he chose.

But under modern conditions all this has changed. The change is due partly to the social and economic evolution of the United States, partly to the altered conditions of transportation, and partly to the changed character of the immigrants themselves.

Whatever the causes, the fact is conspicuous that the immigrant of to-day does not necessarily experience any assimilating influences as a result of residence for five years, or fifteen years, or fifty years. The typical immigrant lives in a compact, distinctive colony virtually as foreign as the land from which he came. He carries on his day's business and pleasure in his own tongue, he attends religious services of the same sort as before his voyage, he reads a newspaper in his native language, he eats the food, plays the games, and dreams the dreams of his homeland. His contacts with Americans are limited almost exclusively to business relationships, and even in those he is much more likely to deal with immigrants of an earlier period than with true Americans. Under such conditions, why should the mere fact of residence upon soil called American or in a community located within the American boundaries produce within him the spiritual transformation that is assimilation? There is no reason why it should, and every reason why it should not, no matter how long extended.

The same situation holds with reference to the expedient of witnesses. When the law was framed it was assumed that these witnesses would be themselves true Americans, presumably native born, and that they would be actual friends, or at least acquaintances, of the candidate. They were supposed to be able to testify, out of their own full knowledge, as to the character of the candidate, and to have formed upon independent grounds an actual judgment as to the candidate's fitness to share in American privileges and obligations as they knew them. Such testimony has value. But under present conditions it is the rare alien who could bring in two native-born Americans — at least of what is called the "old American stock" — simply because there are none such whom he knows and who know him, or care enough about him to take the trouble to act as his witnesses. He is forced to rely upon naturalized citizens, usually of his own original nationality, whose claim to speak for America is no better than his own will be when he has gone through the illusive process in which they are to play so important a part. In actual practice, the witnesses are very frequently paid for their services, and are quite commonly professional witnesses who hang about the naturalization courts prepared to testify to the good moral character and attachment to the Constitution of any alien who has a little good American currency in his pocket.

It would of course be unwarranted to assert that five years of residence, and the testimony of two witnesses are never of any value in showing the effect of Americanizing influences. The period of residence has at least a negative meaning; it is quite impossible for any foreigner to have undergone any considerable part of the assimilating process, however favorable

ENFORCED PATRIOTISM

his situation, in less than five years. But under the best of circumstances, these tests are wholly unreliable as a final guarantee of assimilation. This means that there are no factual tests of assimilation at all.

Turning to the second category of tests it is easily seen that they all boil down to the simple assertion on the part of the candidate that he is truly devoted and loyal to the United States and desires to become an American citizen, being willing for that purpose to give up all foreign allegiances and connections. The fact that part of this statement is made under oath may have much or little significance, according to the attitude which the individual candidate has toward the oath. The disturbing fact is that those aliens who are least fitted for American citizenship and who desire it for the most unworthy ulterior motives are just the ones who will be least deterred by the necessity of affirming a falsehood even though it involves perjury. In the case of aliens who are really fit for American citizenship it makes little difference, except for purely technical purposes, whether they swear allegiance or not; in the case of those who are not fit, the oath is somewhat worse than useless.

The conclusion of the matter is that, except for certain palpable tests of race, age, residence, etc., which are either purely mechanical or else lie beyond the control of the candidate, and the elementary requirements of the use of English and the ability to sign one's name, we virtually give American citizenship away for the asking to any one who is willing to swear his allegiance. The adjuration to become an American citizen requires nothing more than to learn English if one does not know it, and then go through the formal process of asking for citizenship. It is true that this process often involves much inconvenience and annoyance and considerable financial sacrifice to the candidate. He must frequently lose several days' pay, spend money for witnesses and traveling expenses, and undergo a large amount of annoyance and worry, much of which serves no useful purpose, is quite unnecessary, and might well be eliminated. The overcoming of these obstacles, at best, simply indicates that the alien wants American citizenship; it tells nothing at all as to why he wants it, or whether he is fitted for it.

Under these conditions, any attempt to urge or coerce the alien into acquiring citizenship is an outrageous travesty upon patriotism. American citizenship should be the highest political prize that the world has to offer. It should be held up before the foreigner as the ultimate, priceless goal of his endeavors, something which America generously offers to bestow upon him when he can demonstrate his complete social, political, and spiritual fitness to receive it. There should not be the slightest suggestion that he may not want it for its own sake. To hawk it about the streets as if it were something that the recipient conferred a favor by taking is the surest way to destroy any valuation that the alien may himself have put upon it.

There is certainly a profound need for a complete revision of our naturalization requirements and procedure. This does not mean simply that it should be made harder to get citizenship. On the contrary it should be as easy as possible for one to get citizenship who is fitted to get it. But there should be established some genuine, searching tests of fitness for citizenship. Just what these tests should be it is not easy to say. They should be based on the fundamental principle that assimilation should precede naturalization. But how can we devise tests of true assimilation? We can set up certain requirements covering some of the outstanding means to assimilation, on the assumption that if the alien is not in possession of these means he can not by any possibility have experienced thorough assimilation. Foremost among these, of course, is the mastery of the English language, already included in the law. It has been proposed that there should be set up a rather elaborate examination, covering civics, history, economics, etc., and that a textbook should be prepared under government auspices presenting the material to be covered in this examination. Some naturalization judges, on their own initiative, already go much beyond the requirements of the law in inquiring into the educational attainments of the candidate, and citizenship classes are abundant in many parts of the country. Textbooks, also, have been prepared by private agencies, some of which contain a set of questions and answers intended to prepare one for the naturalization examination. The data included are such as an intelligent high-school boy could "cram up" on in about an hour, and it is significant that in one of these books the alien is warned to learn each answer in connection with its appropriate question, instead of by number, for the judge might vary the order of asking!

This informational testing is doubtless useful and should be continued and extended, though the danger should be clearly recognized that it has the tendency to sustain the fallacy that assimilation is an educational process. As already stated, all that such examinations can establish is that the candidate has mastered some of the instruments of assimilation.

It is a very different and vastly more difficult thing to devise tests of the emotional and sentimental status of the alien. How can we discover whether he has really caught the spirit of American standards and institutions, whether he has definitely sloughed off all foreign allegiance and affiliation, whether he devoutly loves and is loyal to America? In this connection the statement may be recalled from an earlier page that complete assimilation is virtually impossible for the adult immigrant, no matter how favorably he may have been situated. Shall we go to the extreme, then, and deny naturalization to all foreigners who were more than, say, ten years old when they arrived? This would seem to be a counsel of perfection, and practically unwise. It is probably true that complete assimilation is not absolutely essential to useful citizenship. A long list could be made of valuable American citizens of foreign birth, each one of whom presumably retained to the day of his death a different feeling toward a certain foreign land than what he would have had if he had been born in America. If an alien has undergone such a transformation that his major loyalty, devotion, understanding, and response are bound up with the American nationality, it is probably best that he should be fully adopted into that fellowship.

It is not the purpose of this book to enter into a detailed consideration of salutary changes in the naturalization procedure, but simply to point out the principles which should govern them. Realizing the difficulties of finding a practical expression of these principles, some students of the matter are inclined to fall back on the tangible requirement of residence, raising the period from five to twenty-five years. This is a proposal already hoary with age, having been an integral part of the tenets of the Native American and Know Nothing Parties, or at least of sections of those parties, but it has little to recommend it. It is at best a makeshift, and introduces no new basis of reliance into the situation. If an alien has spent his entire American residence in some foreign colony, twenty-five years are no better than five. On the other hand, if an alien has been so favorably situated that he has really become assimilated in five or ten years it is useless and unfair to make him wait any longer for his papers. What we need are genuine tests of assimilation, and only by diligent study and search can they be found. In the meantime, we should remember that citizenship confers not only privileges and opportunities, but also responsibilities and powers. Naturalization opens the way to participation in the management of America.[1] It should be perfectly clear that an unassimilated foreigner is not less dangerous, but more dangerous, after he has become a citizen than he was before. The remedy for the perils of great unassimilated population groups is not hasty, arbitrary naturalization, but genuine assimilation and the restriction of the groups to the minimum size. To urge the alien to become an American citizen on pain of deportation or any other penalty is like threatening the newly appointed office boy with the loss of his job if he does not become a member of the Board of Directors within a specified time.

[1] The actual voting power is, of course, conferred by the individual States.

CHAPTER X

The Meaning of America

UNDERLYING all the detailed errors and shortcomings of the Americanization Movement was one fundamental fallacy — the fallacy of assuming that assimilation can be produced by any deliberate, purposeful, artificial measures whatsoever. The magnitude of this fallacy can be appreciated only in the light of a thorough comprehension of the means by which assimilation actually does take place. These have only been suggested hitherto, and now must be considered at some length.

As has already been stated, nationality in the individual is an acquired characteristic which he gets from the group. How the group itself gets its distinctive nationality is an intricate, almost mysterious problem in sociological research which need not detain us in this connection. Every individual must be nationalized; the German is Germanized, the Italian Italianized, and the American Americanized. This process of nationalization begins immediately after birth and continues throughout life. It is automatic and irresistible. No individual can avoid being assimilated into the nationality into which he is born and in which he continues to reside, for the simple reason that the forces of assimilation begin to play upon him while he is still nothing more than an impressionable unit of social protoplasm, and so the basic traits of nationality are deeply implanted in him long before he has developed sufficient will power to exercise any independent action in the matter.

As has been shown, the channels through which the nationalizing influences flow include practically all the points of contact at which the individual touches his social group, beginning with the family and extending on through the whole range of human institutions and relationships. The only differences between the assimilation of the native and the assimilation of the foreigner are to be found in the age at which the forces of a given nationality begin to play upon a certain individual and the nature of the forces to which he is subjected. In the case of the native, under ordinary conditions, there is only one nationality involved, and that one begins to exert its full influence from the very beginning of life. In the case of the foreign immigrant one nationality has already produced its effect before his arrival, and the new nationality must start where the other left off. Furthermore, in the second place, the average immigrant is not immediately after his arrival — nor in fact ever — brought into intimate contact with the full array of nationalizing agencies as is the native. It is this universal lack of natural contacts which

THE MEANING OF AMERICA

led the sponsors of the Americanization Movement to seek to supply some artificial substitutes.

But there can be no substitutes for the genuine forces of assimilation. The only way in which any individual can be nationalized is to live in the nationality in question. The only way in which any person, native or foreigner, can be Americanized is to live in America. The great questions are, then: Does the average immigrant live in America? If not, where does he live? Can he be made to live in America through the operation of any programs, special institutions, or purposeful social devices of any kind? What is America?

In discussions of immigration, speakers who pose as champions of a "liberal" policy may frequently be heard to declare, "The only true Americans are the Red Indians. All the rest of us are immigrants, or the descendants of immigrants." This is a very clever remark, and is always good for at least one round of applause from any audience. But like most clever remarks it justifies a somewhat critical scrutiny.

Just what does it mean to say that the only true Americans are the Red Indians? If they are, what are the rest of us? What is there in common between what was here when the Indians held undisputed sway, and all that goes by the name American to-day? Just one thing — a section of the earth's surface. To say that the Indians are the only true Americans means that what constitutes an American is ancient residence upon a certain territory, which was not even called America until after the white men discovered it. And even on this basis it is difficult to see why the Indians have any better claim to the honored title than the later arrivals, for they themselves are the descendants of wanderers who came from somewhere else. According to this clever saying America is a piece of land, and nothing more. In this case Americanization is either impossible — if you are not a Red Indian you can not possibly make yourself one — or else it consists merely in taking up residence upon this particular piece of land, and any foreigner is Americanized as soon as he disembarks from the vessel that brought him. There are probably very few, however, who would care to limit the definition of America in any such way as this.

What then is America? Some of the discussions of the subject seem to imply that America is a group of people, bound together into a unit by a complex of social ties. Any one who is a member of this group is a part of America, and so all that is necessary to become Americanized is to make one's self a part of this group. But if this is the correct interpretation, then every foreigner is Americanized as soon as he attaches himself in an organic way to this group. So stated, this interpretation also appears as a palpable absurdity. America is not merely an aggregation of people.

THE MEANING OF AMERICA

Sometimes America is spoken of as if it were a political unit, a sovereign State. In that case, an American is one who is an authoritative member of that political unit, and to be Americanized means to obtain admission to the political rights of this government. This conception evidently runs closely parallel to the mental processes of those who urge naturalization as a means of assimilation. But, as has already been pointed out, the War showed all too clearly that there were many persons who had been admitted to full political participation in the country's life whom nobody in those days of stress would have dreamed of calling American. America is something more than a governmental organization.

There remains just one conception of America which at all measures up to the deep-seated, subconscious image which the name suggests. America is a nationality, and fortunately also a nation. America is a spiritual reality. It is a body of ideas and ideals, traditions, beliefs, customs, habits, institutions, standards, loyalties, a whole complex of cultural and moral values. Many efforts have been made to define America by cataloguing these diversified features. It is a difficult thing to do, and fortunately unnecessary for an adequate understanding of the nature of assimilation. No two persons would name exactly the same traits as essential to Americanism; yet there would be a long list upon which practically every one would agree: such things as business honesty, respect for womanhood, inventiveness, political independence, physical cleanliness, good sportsmanship, and others less creditable, such as worship of success, material-mindedness, boastfulness, etc. It is no denial of the reality of this interpretation of America to point out that very few individuals could be found who embody all these traits, or even most of them, in their own persons and character. This is obviously true, just as it is true that it is impossible to find any individual who conforms perfectly to the type of the race to which he belongs. But the race type exists, nevertheless, and America exists, even though there be found not one individual who perfectly represents it. As already emphasized, nationality is a mass reality not a personal possession.

The true Americans, then, are those who embody most completely in their individual characters, and taken as a mass embody perfectly, the spiritual traits and qualities that make up the American nationality. It is not a question of birth, ancestry, or race. A person may be born within sight of Plymouth Rock, of old colonial stock, and be much less an American than one whose parents brought him here in an immigrant ship a quarter of a century ago. American fellowship and affiliation are natural, easy, and largely unconscious for one who has always lived in America. They are an achievement for one whose origin is foreign. But America is one and the same for all.

THE MEANING OF AMERICA

America was not found ready-made and waiting on this side of the Atlantic by the white settlers who first set foot on the new continent. America was brought to this continent, brought by the Pilgrim Fathers in the Mayflower, brought in the dozens of frail vessels which carried the forerunners of a new people and a new nation. America was brought over as a tender plant, ill defined and simple, with little indication of the form into which it was to grow. It was planted in the congenial soil of a new land. It was watered by the blood and the sweat and the tears of those who brought it, and of the generations that came after them. And because it was a vigorous, hardy plant with a unique and sturdy vitality, because it was well adapted to the new environment in which it had been set out, and because it was devotedly cherished by those who had faith in its future it took root, and grew, and developed into that magnificent creation that we call America to-day.

So America is a living, vital thing existing in the minds and hearts of true Americans. Closely associated with this spiritual reality is the common possession of a favored section of the earth's surface, the consolidation into an effective social group, and the participation in organized governmental activities. But America is more than any one of these, more than all of them put together.

To live in America, then, is to live in the atmosphere of these immaterial standards and values, to possess them in one's own character, and to be possessed by them. This means to live in close, spontaneous, daily contact with genuine Americans. For the native-born American of American ancestry, as already stated, this is natural and automatic. What is it for the foreign immigrant?

In the discussion of naturalization it was stated that the average immigrant of a century ago could hardly help coming in contact with true Americans and participating in genuine American life. To-day, just the reverse is true. The typical immigrant of the present does not really live in America at all, but, from the point of view of nationality, in Italy, Poland, Czecho-Slovakia, or some other foreign country. Let us look into the causes of this situation, and examine the barriers that keep the foreigner out of America.

The first cause of the change is found in a modification in the American nationality itself. During the century and a half of our independent national life we have developed from a simply organized, agricultural community into an elaborate, complicated, mechanical, and industrial society. The whole quality of our group life has altered correspondingly. Instead of homogeneity and essential equality have come heterogeneity and class distinctions. At the beginning of the nineteenth century the character of the typical American community was much like that of the mediæval village, of which it has been

THE MEANING OF AMERICA

said that its distinctive feature was that "every one knew everything about everybody else." Class differentiation existed only in the rudimentary stage. The relation of employer and employee existed, but it was developed only on a small scale, and was distinctly personal in character. It was typified by the association between the farmer and his "hired man." The latter was just as self-respecting and often of just as good family as the former. The hired man worked side by side with his employer in the fields on terms of essential equality, ate his meals with the family, and on Sunday evening put on his "store clothes" and took the daughter of the house to church. The situation in which the employee never met his boss, and did not know his appearance or even his name, would have been almost inconceivable. A German visitor, traveling through the United States about the middle of the last century, commented on the remarkable independence of the working classes. He stated that if one went to make a call, and inquired of the servant who answered the door, "Is your master in?" he was likely to get an indignant look with the reply, "I have no master. Perhaps you mean Mr. So-and-so." He also observed that an offer of a tip — *mirabile dictu* — was invariably refused with scorn.

The contrast between this picture and the present situation scarcely needs comment. The employee, or wage-earning, class is now a distinct and separate element in the population. While there is a theoretical possibility, and not infrequent actual examples, of moving up out of this class, the feasibility or likelihood of such an outcome is so slight as to exercise very little influence on the general situation. Workers to-day are characteristically employed not by the boss himself, or even by his personal representative, but by an official who is himself an employee, and often not much superior in caliber to the applicant. What is true in the industrial relation is equally true in the associations of religion, the family, sports, art, and even politics. Much as we dislike to admit it, sharp class differentiations have become an integral feature of American life, and the contacts of the lower with the higher classes (in the accepted meaning of those terms) are becoming yearly more tenuous.

All this has serious implications enough for the American population itself. But it is decidedly more significant in the case of the immigrant. For the great majority of immigrants come here as members of the wage-earning class, and most of them remain so. Most of them, also, are poor. So in their efforts to penetrate the stream of Americanizing influences they have to face the handicap not only of alien origin and character, but also of an inferior economic status and absolute poverty. To cap the climax, the differentiation of occupations has gone so far that to-day a large number of callings are almost completely given over to foreign workers, often of specific national groups. They have become "Wop labor", "Hunkie labor", "Kike labor", etc. Consequently the foreigner, not to speak of associating with "upper class" Americans, does not even have the opportunity of mingling with genuine Americans in his own walk of life. The typical immigrant of to-day is not only hired, paid, and fired by a person scarcely less foreign than himself, but he also works side by side and shoulder to shoulder with a group of persons who are usually "greeners" like himself and quite frequently members of his own nationality.

A second great cause of the change in the conditions of assimilation is found in the altered type of the immigrants themselves, as already pointed out in the distinction between the old and the new immigration. The typical immigrants of the first one hundred years of our national life came from the same nationalities as the ancestors of the native Americans. The change that they had to undergo in order to be assimilated was the same change that the ancestors of their associates had passed through. Herein lies one of the significant applications of the fact, established at some length in earlier pages, that the American nationality was in all essential respects closely akin to the English nationality, and not far remote from the nationalities of the countries of northwestern Europe. To-day, the immigrants represent as diverse and inharmonious nationalities as are to be found among all the branches of the white race. The transformation necessary for assimilation is therefore both more sweeping and more difficult. Even if our modern immigrants had equal opportunities of contact with genuine Americans to those of two or three generations ago — a supposition, as we have seen, contrary to fact — they would still have a vastly more arduous road to travel before they could justly claim the title "American." Faced, as they are, with virtually insuperable barriers to association, they find assimilation hardly even a remote possibility.

One of the most characteristic of the National Americanization Committee's "Pay Envelope Series" reads as follows:

AMERICA

You Live in America
You Work in America
Why Not Be a Part of America?
Citizenship Makes You a Part of America

We have seen how viciously false is the statement that citizenship makes the foreigner a part of America. Equally false is the assertion that the foreigner lives and works in America, and the implication that the act of becoming a "part of America" is — to use the vernacular — strictly "up to him." The only way to become a part of America is to live in America for an extended period of time. But the immigrant does not live in America. So what is he to do, and what are we to do?

The outstanding fact in this connection is that as a result of a century and a half of immigration there have been built up within the physical boundaries of what is called America extensive and deeply intrenched offshoots of numerous foreign nationalities. These are most conspicuous, and probably most frequent, in our great cities, and any one who has participated in any form of social case work has inevitably become familiar with them. But they exist in equally well-developed forms in the less crowded sections of the country devoted to agriculture, mining, and other extractive pursuits. In a certain section of Nebraska, a generation ago, one could drive for miles without meeting an adult who could speak English, and "Dutch Bohunk" was a customary epithet of opprobrium among the native American children of the town. Similar situations exist all over the land, furnishing conclusive refutation of the common argument that "distribution" can be relied upon to solve all the evils of immigration.

These "foreign colonies", as they are commonly called, are living evidences of the tenacity of nationality. They show how vigorously every individual clings to his own original national traits, how choice and dear they seem to him, and how difficult it is for him to change them even if he wishes. There are many sections of the United States in which even the third generation of immigrants does not speak English.

The persistence of nationality, and the revolutionary nature of the transformation involved in a change of nationality, can hardly be comprehended by one who has never been called upon to undergo such a process. For the average native-born American, whose life has been spent continuously in the congenial atmosphere of his own nationality, perhaps there is no better means of illustrating the nature of assimilation than by considering the change that is involved in a movement from one part of the United States to another, such as tens of thousands of Americans have experienced. Take, for example, the case "of a young man who has been brought up in a strictly Puritanical community, and, in his early twenties, let us say, moves to a community with a less rigid code. He has been trained not to play cards, not to dance, not to smoke, perhaps not to attend the theater or play pool or billiards. He has been made to believe that these things are wrong, and so he does actually regard them as wrong. Yet in his new environment he sees the very best people doing all of these things without any compunction or even any sense of their being questionable. Their code is different from his. Such a person goes through a very difficult and trying transition period. If he has a good intellect and if his moral sentiments are healthy and sound, he usually works his way out

THE MEANING OF AMERICA

all right. But in the meantime his pathway is surrounded with many pitfalls."[1] Even in a country as closely unified as the United States there are many varying social environments. The change from one to another is always a soul-trying experience, yet it is as nothing compared to that which every immigrant must undergo who actually moves into America.

Illustrations of the nature of the contrasts between diverse nationalities, and the difficulty of harmonizing them, might be multiplied almost indefinitely. Some have already been given. A few more may be added to emphasize the true nature of the experience which we demand of the immigrant when we call upon him to be assimilated.

Two young men, an Englishman and an American, both teachers in schools in a Turkish city and therefore familiar with a variety of national institutions, were sitting at one of the outdoor tables in front of a café in Athens. There passed by an officer of the Greek army in uniform in the company of a civilian apparently of humble status. The young Englishman was struck by the incident, and commented upon it.

"You would never see anything like that in England."

"Why not?" inquired the American.

"Because in England the officers come from the aristocratic families, and would not condescend to

[1] Quoted from the author's "Elements of Social Science", page 115.

walk on the streets with a common man. It's a very good system too, because it creates a profound respect for the officers on the part of the enlisted men."

"But it can not be nearly as effective as the American system," said the other, "where the officers are chosen for ability or distinguished conduct. That is a much more powerful basis for respect than mere birth."

The point was argued at length, with of course no change in the ideas of either disputant. Now the ancestors of the American and the Britisher might well have been kinsmen and neighbors in some English village not so many generations ago, yet their views on this fundamental subject were as wide apart as the poles. Ask yourself, proud descendant of old Pilgrim lineage, how long you would have to live in England before you became convinced that the system of a hereditary aristocracy was a sounder basis for military gradation than individual ability and achievement. Yet in other respects, these two young men were vastly closer to each other than they were to their Greek and Armenian pupils, who simply could not conceive, for instance, how their teacher could innocently take a walk in the country alone with a young woman.

One of the recent characteristic expressions of the American nationality is the attempt to secure the suppression of the use of alcoholic beverages by national legislation. It is a unique and courageous adventure, and the American people certainly ought to have the opportunity to try it out, in accordance with established American institutions and constitutional procedure, without the interference of millions of persons whose traditional attitude toward both the use of alcoholic drinks and constitutional and representative government is so distinctly foreign that they can not possibly even comprehend the character and spirit of this undertaking. Yet there can be no doubt that the alien elements in this country form one of the most serious obstacles, not to the success of the Prohibition Movement — upon which genuine Americans hold very divergent opinions — but to the legitimate prosecution of the experiment in democratic government which the Eighteenth Amendment and the Volstead Act represent. In spite of all that is said about the "machinations of an organized minority", there can be no doubt that these two measures were carried out in strict conformity to the established legal procedure of the United States. But the enforcement of them is immeasurably hampered by the activities of countless individuals who are completely indifferent to American institutions and completely unresponsive to American public opinion. The situation has been humorously described in the following words: "Many of these people simply fail to get the idea of prohibition. Thousands of them think it was put into force by executive decree of President Wilson. I have heard them talk about it for hours and advocate a twenty-four hour national strike in protest, believing that thus they can force President Harding to rescind the decree. To try to explain the theory of prohibition to a group of Italian workmen is very much like trying to explain to you, the reader, that in Siberia people walk on their ears. In other words, it sounds interesting, but it does not 'get over.' A friend of mine, a Red Cross worker during the war, related to me his futile effort to explain American prohibition to an Italian Senator in Italy. The Senator listened with attention for three quarters of an hour and then asked 'But what kind of wine do they drink now?' The fact that they are not supposed to drink wine at all simply failed to register with him. It was inconceivable. People of this type, who are otherwise law-abiding and patriotic and well-intentioned, protect bootleggers and otherwise violate the Volstead Act with the same faith in the justice of their actions that a group of Middle Western Americans would have in evading a law that prohibited them from planting corn." [1]

It is significant that most of the bootleggers, at least as far as one can judge from ordinary evidence — statistics do not seem to be available — appear to be foreigners. Doubtless a handsome proportion, if not the majority, of their patrons are native-born Americans. But this does not alter the case. It

[1] C. T. Crowell, "How Prohibition Works", *Independent and Weekly Review*, Jan. 14, 1922.

seems that one of the features of the American nationality in its immediate phase is a nice distinction between patronizing a bootlegger and being a bootlegger. If there were not abundant non-Americans who were quite willing to be bootleggers, the trade would almost certainly fall off markedly. It can not be purely by chance that a map of "wetness" in the United States is almost a replica of a map showing the distribution of the foreign-born. All of this, be it remembered, is not an argument for or against Prohibition, but an illustration of the difficulty of expressing the national will in an experimental policy when national unity does not exist.

These special national loyalties and affiliations persist for many generations, even when the individual descendants of the original immigrants are almost completely assimilated. Group feeling as expressed in group pride is one of the most enduring of all human sentiments. Mention has already been made of the elaborate exposition called "America's Making." This was conceived as a means of promoting a better understanding, not only between Americans and foreigners, but also between the various groups of foreigners — an aspect of the Americanization problem, by the way, all too frequently neglected. Doubtless many useful results were accomplished in this direction. But behind the scenes, according to the newspaper reports, some lively and incongruous displays of group jealousy marred the serene atmosphere of the enterprise. These clashes were largely caused by rival claims as to the group affiliation of certain prominent Americans of various early periods. It is significant that antagonism was sharpest not among the representatives of the new immigration, who are presumably least completely assimilated, but among the Scotch and the Irish. An Irishman, checking over the list of notables displayed in the Scotch booth, was outraged to find a number of persons included whom he claimed as pure Irish. The chairman of the Scotch group, however, maintained that "the Scotch-Irish of the north of Ireland always have been and always will be Scotch regardless of where they make their home." The Welsh also entered the controversy by claiming President Monroe, who was listed in both the Welsh and the Scotch booths. Even as these words are being written the newspapers print an account of a journey of the President of the United States halfway across the continent to take part in a great "Norse" celebration, in commemoration of the completion of one hundred years of Norwegian settlement in this country. Doubtless the celebrants are all loyal and patriotic, yet the vivid consciousness of their foreign origin is a definite factor in American national disunity, just as it is in the case of any other group similarly inspired.

All of this may seem very trivial and inconsequential to the native American who has never been thrown into the stress of conflicting nationalities. But nationality is largely a matter of things that are in themselves trivial, but nevertheless have a profound effect in creating group feeling. A whimsical presentation of this truth has been given by Mr. Clarence Day, Jr., in a sketch which deserves to be quoted in full, but of which this paragraph must stand as representative.

"'Why is it,'" the old explorer was wondering, "'that men care so for trifles? Even death and danger won't stop us, or make us less fussy. In a country where a man knows that he's likely to be killed any day, in the middle of his career, he ought to have a little sense of proportion. But life's not safe a minute in Kiboa, for instance, and have they any sense? Not a bit. People there are exactly as finicky as everywhere else. They spend most of their time being preoccupied with meaningless nothings. I did more for those Kiboans than I have ever done for any tribe since — I stamped out two fever epidemics and taught them how to build mill wheels — and yet, at their great banquet to celebrate the lives I had saved, they were horrified because I used the wrong stick to eat with at table. There were two sticks, a prong and a flat one. I ate peas with the flat one. I should have used the prong. Well, that ended me. They still tried to be grateful, but it was painful to them — I had turned out low caste.'"[1]

[1] The *New Republic*, October 18, 1922, page 198.

It would be the gravest mistake to conclude, however, that nationality is all a matter of nonessentials or superficialities. There should, indeed, be no doubt on that point at this stage of our discussion. Nationality includes all the deepest, dearest, most inalienable, and most unquestioned elements in the social inheritance of every individual. This can be appreciated by recalling that the moral code itself is a part of nationality. It is true that there are certain fundamental resemblances among the moral codes of all civilized peoples, and even of barbarous or savage peoples, just as there are basic physical resemblances among all the races of man. But this is only because, nationally as well as racially, men are much more alike than they are different. Nevertheless, it is the differences that divide men into groups, and differences in moral codes are as nearly insuperable as any barrier that exists. During the unreflective and uncritical years of character formation the authority of the moral code of one's own particular group is absolute. Consequently, by the time one reaches an age of analytical comparison the sway of one's own code has become so firmly established that it is almost impossible, by the exercise of any processes of reasoning, to emancipate one's self from it. You may convince yourself that in some particular respect the code of France, or Turkey, or Japan is higher, or more rational, or more conducive to human well-being than your own. But it is quite a different thing to make yourself feel comfortable when you begin to pattern your conduct after that code. A remarkable illustration of these truths was furnished by the case of the young Albanian who killed his countryman, Essad Pasha, in Paris in 1920. In the course of the trial the fact was brought out that Essad Pasha had previously been instrumental in causing the death of the father of his slayer. According to Albanian law and social usage it was not only the right, but also the duty, of the younger man to pursue the man who had killed his father until he had accomplished his death. The remarkable feature of the case is that although the crime was committed on French soil, and the case was tried before a French court, the decision was that the young Albanian was governed by the Albanian code, and hence in committing what we would call a murder he not only *thought* he was right but he *was* right. He was therefore acquitted.

The process of Americanization, then, for the immigrant is infinitely more difficult than for the native because the former, during the years before his arrival in the United States, has already acquired more or less completely a foreign nationality. This nationality is dissimilar in most respects, and absolutely contradictory and inconsistent in many respects, to the American nationality. Yet to the foreigner it is his natural and authoritative spiritual tradition and social environment. He may hold a critical attitude toward certain aspects of it, just as most Americans are dissatisfied with some phases of the American nationality, but taken as a whole it represents to him truth, beauty, goodness, morality, justice, propriety, efficiency, custom, order, and — home. Let the critical and self-satisfied American of native birth reflect that in the process of Americanization this whole spiritual endowment must be abandoned, and another taken in its place, and it may help him dimly to perceive how tragic, how soul-wracking must be the experience of assimilation, though probably no one who has not actually gone through it can appreciate the stress and tragedy involved.

CHAPTER XI

THE MAKING OF AMERICANS

ONE of the gravest dangers involved in this transformation lies in the fact that the foreigner who is eager for assimilation will try to adopt the behavior of his new group before he has acquired the inner feeling that normally accompanies and justifies that behavior. In attempting to revolutionize his conduct and ideas in an essentially artificial way, he lacks the necessary balance wheel. He is incapable of distinguishing between fundamentals and superficialities. In constantly going counter to his previous notions he is likely to do violence to his conscience and his moral sense. This is doubtless one of the reasons for the notable lawlessness and instability of the second generation of immigrants. They throw over the old before they are competent to take on the new. It is a very risky thing to try when in Rome to do as the Romans do, because you can not possibly feel as the Romans feel.

We come back, then, to the central questions: What can the immigrant do, and what can the native do, to promote Americanization?

As far as the immigrant is concerned, he has already made the first essential move by coming to this country. He has stepped through the door that we have opened to him, often in the face of great difficulties and at heavy sacrifice to himself. But this is by no means enough. He must devoutly wish to be Americanized. It is true enough that assimilation can not be accomplished by an act of the will, but there is nevertheless such a thing as the will to assimilate. If this exists, the immigrant will eagerly seize every opportunity to extend the sphere of his activities a little nearer the center of American life, to catch the spirit of the real America. Unfortunately, this state of mind is conspicuous by its absence on the part of a considerable portion of our immigrant population. One part of this group is composed of those who have come here primarily to share in the economic advantages of this favored land. They have little interest in the social or political features of the American nationality. Many of them do not expect to remain here permanently, but to return to a life of ease and respect in their native lands as soon as they have accumulated enough American dollars to enable them to do so. With reference to such as these, all that we need say is, the sooner they carry out their purpose to return, and the fewer of their kind who come to take their places, the better.

A more significant — and probably more dangerous — type of foreigner who lacks the will to assimilate includes those who, on high intellectual and cultural grounds, oppose assimilation because of the inroads it makes into the strength of their own original nationalities. These persons are so deeply impressed with the value of the distinct cultures which they represent that they regard the subtraction of each individual from these cultures as a definite loss to mankind. There is a considerable propaganda in existence in the United States at the present time designed to encourage immigrants to oppose and resist assimilation. This is most conspicuous among our Hebrew population. Cases have been numerous in the last few months where Rabbis and other prominent Jewish leaders have urged their people to remain distinct, and to strive to become constantly more Jewish. One of the most convincing presentations of this point of view is found in an article by Rabbi Joel Blau, entitled "The Modern Pharisee" in the *Atlantic Monthly* for January, 1922. It abounds in such stirring passages as these:

"But the Modern Pharisee knows that these dissimilarities hold the secret of Jewish individuality. Upon this knowledge he stands four-square, neither pleading nor apologizing. He has nothing to hide, nothing to gloss over. He calmly faced all attacks upon the citadel of Jewish personality, no matter whence they emanate: from foe or friend, from the Christian world, or from his own Sadducee brother. *The broad way of assimilation — one might call it the Jewish 'Main Street' — he would not tread: he knows too well the egregious folly of assimilation.*[1] Moses Hess, one of the first writers on Zionism in the last century, tells amusingly in his startling *Rom und Jerusalem* of the son of a rich German-Jewish banker, who would stand in front of his mirror for hours on end, desperately endeavoring to iron out the Semitic kinks of his hair. But, straight hair or curly locks, can any Jew ever hope to straighten out the 'kinks' of his oriental soul? This oriental soul the Modern Pharisee claims as his birthright, not to be traded away for the contents of any pot — even though it be the Melting-Pot."

Sentiments such as these, baldly expressed by the foreigners in our midst, are likely to arouse the fierce ire of the one hundred per cent. American, and elicit a bitter condemnation not only of those who express them, but of all who feel them, however silently. They should not do so. They are perfectly natural and wholly defensible sentiments. They are, as has been pointed out, exactly the sentiments that we admire when displayed by Americans in foreign lands. They are patriotism. Any alien who feels these emotions toward his own nationality should not be blamed for it. Neither should he be blamed for coming, temporarily or permanently, to a country where he thinks he can enjoy wider personal opportunities, just as Americans go freely wherever fortune beckons. The ones who should be blamed are the Americans them-

[1] Italics mine. Author.

selves who allow patriotic foreigners to come in great numbers, and to stay when it is clear that the object of their patriotism is not likely to be shifted to America. Such persons, as will be shown, constitute an undeniable menace to American national stability. This does not imply that we want unpatriotic foreigners. They are likely to be not better, but worse, than the others. If they have not been loyal to the land of their birth they are not likely to be loyal to the land of their adoption. It means that we want very few foreigners of any kind. The wholesome place for the display of patriotism is at home. The difficulty in the case of the Jews is that they have no home. They have no nation to the upbuilding of which they can devote their restless activities, and about the future of which they can entwine their ardent aspirations. Consequently they are driven to seek to perpetuate their own nationality in the midst of other nationalities. This is wholly defensible from the point of view of the Jews. It is intolerable from the point of view of the other nationalities. The outstanding utility of the Zionist movement is not in providing an outlet for large surplus Jewish populations, but in furnishing a focus of Jewish devotion and service which may help to reduce the intense particularism of the Jews in other lands.

There are, however, in our midst at the present time, and there will come in future years in spite of the new restrictive law, millions of foreigners who are destined to remain as a part of the population of the United States. Upon them rests a definite obligation to play their full part in promoting Americanization. If it were possible to devise tests of arriving immigrants, or of aliens of long residence in this country, which would reveal the real state of their minds with respect to their eagerness for assimilation and their readiness to do their part, we would be quite justified in excluding or deporting, as the case might be, all who did not measure up to a high standard. Such tests being impossible, we must take it for granted that all aliens who are here, or who come here, with the expressed intention of remaining permanently, are doing their best to experience Americanization, and we must act on the assumption, which is near enough the truth, that the principal practical obstacles to Americanization are set by the inherent conditions of the assimilative process, and the particular features of American life, and so are to be removed, if at all, by the efforts of Americans themselves.

The first thing to recognize is that assimilation is partly a quantitative problem. The possibilities and probabilities of the immigrant's having a chance to live in America are greatly enhanced if there are not too many of him. If there are not enough foreigners of a given nationality in a given city to form a fairly self-contained and self-sufficient colony, there will be no colony. If the immigrant can find no one to associate with except Americans, he must associate with Americans. Consequently, the restrictive aspects of the new immigration law have a profound and salutary bearing on the assimilation problem of the immediate and more distant future. There are good grounds for believing that this limitation of numbers came just in the nick of time. A few years of the voluminous immigration that would have poured into this country if there had been no restriction would almost certainly have worked disaster to the American nationality that could never have been repaired.

In the second place, it may well be borne in mind that the problem of assimilation differs greatly with different nationalities. In general terms, those foreign nationalities that are most like the American create the least problems of assimilation, first because the process of Americanization is simpler and swifter in their case, and second because the deficiencies of Americanization that persist are much less likely to be dangerous than in the case of more remote nationalities. For instance, it is sometimes asserted that the Englishman is one of the hardest of all foreigners to completely assimilate in the United States. The answer is, that it does not make a great amount of difference whether the Englishman is fully assimilated or not. Whatever remains of his original nationality will be so much like the American that it is not likely to cause much disturbance.

Herein lies the great value of the group-selective features of the new immigration law. This piece of legislation is so designed that when it gets into full operation a total annual immigration of 150,000 from the countries of the eastern hemisphere will be distributed exactly in accordance with the national origins of the total American population of 1920. This means that, as far as immigration is concerned, the racial dilution of the American stock is to be checked and the strain of accommodating ourselves to constant arrivals of representatives of foreign nationalities will be reduced to a minimum. The Immigration Act of 1924 may justly be regarded as one of the most influential and far-reaching pieces of legislation ever enacted in human history.

But in spite of this new legal situation, there remains a tremendous problem of Americanization, the solution of which rests chiefly upon the American people themselves. A preliminary step in this solution consists in eliminating once and for all the habit of mind that condemns the alien for his nonassimilation, and expresses itself in many forms of blame and censure. We must not only recognize that the foreigner cannot voluntarily assimilate himself, but we must also remember that the process of assimilation, even at its best, involves a long period of transition, when the foreigner is neither one thing nor the other. Nationalities are vital only when complete and whole. The different phases of two diverse nationalities are almost certain to be largely incompatible with each other. One cannot be unreservedly loyal to two different fatherlands. Nor is it possible to make the transfer of allegiance at one sudden jump. As already suggested, there were many German-Americans, and probably are to-day, who were exactly what the name implies — neither German nor American. And so with every other hyphenated nationality. This feature of assimilation will doubtless prove very trying to Americans, but it must be immeasurably more trying to the foreigner himself. Since it is unavoidable, it should be recognized that the alien who is passing through this stage merits every possible sympathy, allowance, and assistance. Everything is to be gained by shortening the period as much as possible.

As a means of promoting this transition every educational device which will help the immigrant to know America, and every social expedient which will help him to live in America, should be encouraged. Instead of preaching to the immigrant about the duty of loving America, Americans should recognize their twofold duty in the matter. The first part of this duty is to see that America shall be lovable. We can not love an object unless we know it, but no amount of knowledge will create affection unless the object itself be found lovable. Unfortunately, much as we dislike to confess it, many aspects of the America which the immigrant comes to know do not impress him as lovable at all. One of the most depressing and disheartening features of the recent immigration situation is the frequency with which foreigners return to their native land quite disillusioned as to the beauties and glories of America. One can observe these emigrants searching the store of expletives and epithets which makes up so large a part of their English vocabulary to find an adequate expression of the scorn and contumely in which they hold this Land of (broken) Promise. We may console ourselves with the thought — which is probably largely accurate — that this is because they have never come to know the real America. It is just another expression of the truth, so repeatedly emphasized, that the average foreigner does not work and does not live in America. His residence on the soil of America is passed in contact with the tattered fringes and unsightly seams of the real American fabric. He thinks he knows America. In fact, he has seen only a caricature of it. His life experiences, like his daily reading, might be characterized by the conceptions of the comic strip cartoonist, except that his experience is likely to be much less comic than tragic. This point is pathetically illustrated by the young Slavic woman, cited by Miss Balch, who, on her return to her native land, declared that the people in America who spoke English the best were the colored people; or the Croatian laborer who said that he "did not know how to talk in

English to *ladies.*" Such was the America that they knew.

The *sine qua non*, then, of Americanization is that America should be lovable. This involves the eradication of those features of the American nationality that arouse the scorn, derision, and hatred of the foreigner — elements of social injustice, of political corruption, of relentless commercialism, of a thousand and one things, alas! which the native American sees but recognizes as mere unsightly excrescences on the body of the true America, but which to the alien represent America itself. The problem of Americanization is at bottom just one phase of the great problem of social regeneration.

But granting that America is become so attractive that any one really knowing it can not help loving it, the second part of the task remains of helping the immigrant to know America. This means, in the first place, helping him to know about America. This is the legitimate field for all those activities and agencies which have been and are included in the conventional conception of Americanization. These are the means for opening up the channels of assimilation. Obviously, the first essential is a fluent use of the English language, which is the accepted medium for the communication of ideas in America. In this connection the problem of the foreign language press calls for consideration. The extent and importance of this institution was little realized until it was thrown into sharp relief by the exigencies of the War. Probably few people even to-day realize how voluminous and diversified are the periodicals printed in foreign languages, nor how wide their circulation. According to the latest figures there are over one thousand different periodicals printed in nearly forty different languages in the United States. There is some difference of opinion as to whether the foreign language press as a whole tends to promote or retard Americanization. On the one hand it is urged that if the alien could not get a paper or magazine in his own language he would be stimulated to learn English, and that the news and editorials presented in a foreign medium are certain to be biased and misrepresentative of American life. On the other hand, it is asserted that it is better to read in a foreign language than not to read at all, and that the use of a foreign language paper is the best preparation and inducement for the eventual mastery of English. Of much less importance is the argument sometimes advanced that these papers are used as the medium for deliberate anti-American propaganda. Wherever the arguments may lead, the fact is that these papers are here, and probably here to stay for some time at least. The task is to make the best possible use of them in promoting an understanding of American institutions, and it is encouraging to note that vigorous and well-conceived efforts in this direction are being carried out by at least one agency created largely for this specific purpose.

In addition to a knowledge of English, it is important that the foreigner, adult or child, should receive an educational grounding in all the essential fields included in the education of the native. The educational requirements that we impose upon persons born in America are certainly not greater than those essential for persons born in foreign nationalities. It is worth asking whether one of the tests of assimilation that should precede naturalization might not well be an educational preparation equivalent to the minimum requirements of the American compulsory education system. Just how much of this might be accepted in the form of credits from foreign schools it would be difficult to say. The whole scheme would involve great difficulty, and very likely would prove impracticable in the case of adult immigrants. The task of providing educational facilities and educational inducements for all the millions of adult aliens in this country would be stupendous. But the point serves to emphasize how heavy is the burden of producing even the means of Americanization.

In the case of the children of immigrants, either brought to the United States at an early age or born here, the problem is much simpler. We have our public-school system, and into it are supposed to go all children, native and foreign alike, who fall within certain limits of age and education, unless they receive the equivalent schooling in some other way. If the average citizen were asked to name the chief single Americanization agency he would almost invariably mention the public-school system. He would undoubtedly be right. It is upon the public-school system that our chief reliance is placed, and by the same sort of inverted logic which has already been noticed, it is commonly assumed that it is adequate. We know that there is no other agency equal to the schools in assimilating influence. We recognize that we must have assimilation. Therefore we assume that the public schools are producing assimilation.

An examination of the actual facts leaves a much less reassuring impression. In the first place, a very considerable proportion of the children of foreigners do not attend the public schools, but go to parochial schools, which, whatever their standing as educational agencies, fall far short of the public schools as Americanizing agencies. In the second place, the public schools themselves have been largely de-Americanized as a result of the insupportable burden of foreignness that has been laid upon them. Several years ago one of the foremost pedagogists in the country, commenting upon the breakdown of the American public-school system (which he took as an accepted fact, needing no demonstration) cited immigration as one of the chief causes. On account of the localization of our foreign population in specialized districts it has come about that the very schools which ought to be exercising the greatest assimilating influence have a population of students almost exclusively foreign, and often a large proportion of the teachers are only partly Americanized. Now it is living with Americans, in school as elsewhere, that produces Americanization. The mere fact of studying in a school supported by American taxes and organized on the American system does not produce Americanization if the human elements that really constitute the school are not a part of America.

Most important of all, however, is the fact that the public school is only one of the multitude of assimilating influences to which the child of American parents is exposed from birth up, and which result in making him an American. It is surely absurd to assume that the child of foreign parents can be Americanized by one factor alone. The most important of all the forces which contribute to the nationalization of an individual, as has been shown, is the family. In this particular, not only the foreign-born child, but the native-born child of foreign parents, and sometimes even the representative of the third or fourth generation of immigrant stock, labors under an unavoidable handicap as compared with the child whose parents really belong to America. The child of immigrant parents never lives in a truly American home. The determining impressions which mold his national character during the most impressionable years of his life come not from American, but from foreign, sources. Consequently, even though in other respects his environment is very favorable to assimilation, he will never be quite the same person as if his whole life had been lived in America. So he, in turn, will not be able to furnish a completely representative American home environment to his children. These are the realities that led Professor Ward to say, "The assimilation of an alien civilization . . . can not be accomplished in a single generation, no matter how favorable the conditions may be." [1]

A remarkable concrete illustration of this truth is afforded by the following statement, made by an individual who has the rare capacity to view his own assimilation objectively:

"My ancestors came from England to America in 1635, settling in Middletown, Connecticut. Our branch of the family migrated with the Loyalists to New Brunswick, where I was born and raised. At the age of eighteen I came to New England and have lived here for over thirty years. Preferring not to be a member of any hyphenated society or association, I have purposely joined and rubbed elbows with the members of organizations already established that are typical of American life. That has also been my attitude towards government and society in general, to accept what was already established and fit into my niche as best I could. But notwithstanding the fact that I have always been kindly received,

[1] L. F. Ward, "Applied Sociology", page 109.

THE MAKING OF AMERICANS

added to the advantage of a common heritage, language, traditions, manners and customs (and I might be considered a fair average common denominator), I have not had the feeling of complete absorption into America until within the past few years. If it takes one with all the advantages of an Anglo-Saxon heritage so long to feel assimilated, what hope can there be of assimilating those whose race is also entirely foreign?"

But after all has been done that can be done to help the foreigner know about America, the real problem has hardly been touched. To know about America is not equivalent to knowing America, any more than knowing about Abraham Lincoln is equivalent to knowing Abraham Lincoln.

We come back to the fundamental proposition that since the only way for the foreigner to be Americanized is to live in America the manifest duty of the American with reference to those foreigners whom he has taken the responsibility of admitting is to make it possible for them to live in America. This, it must be stated emphatically, can not be done by any specific activities organized directly for the purpose. The representative of the old native stock is not nationalized by means of pageants, night classes, folk dances, and expositions, and neither can the foreigner be. There is no way to Americanization except the natural one of spontaneous, unartificial, fully rounded participation on terms of unconscious fellowship in all the social relationships which make up the life activities of this elaborate, complicated nation.

Is such participation possible to the foreign immigrant, or, in the majority of cases, to his children? It is dishearteningly obvious that at the present time it does not take place. What are the obstacles that impede it? This question takes us back to a recognition of the fundamental forces of group feeling—racial sympathy and antipathy on the one hand, and national sympathy and antipathy on the other. Association and contact take place spontaneously where group sympathy naturally exists. They have to be established by purposive methods, if at all, where antipathy governs. Among the components of the real America there is, in the very nature of the case, an effective national sympathy. This does not mean that they all feel alike about every detail of nationality, but that they are in essential agreement upon fundamentals, they share a common loyalty, and their divergence on nonessentials is traceable to individual characteristics, not to affiliation with some foreign group. Racially, there is no such complete unity even in America itself. As we have seen, among the representatives of the various white stocks in this country there is probably very little racial antipathy. But the presence of the black element has as yet proved an effective barrier to complete racial sympathy. It is by no means impossible

THE MAKING OF AMERICANS

that this factor may even yet seriously disrupt the American nation.

At this point it should be observed that while racial antipathy is an entirely distinct thing from national antipathy, it nevertheless plays an important part in the problem of assimilation. The reason is simply that racial antipathy, when it exists, forms an additional obstacle to the establishment of those free associations through which assimilation takes place. Assimilation is difficult enough when the only barriers are national. When they are supported and reinforced by active racial feeling the task of assimilation becomes simply impossible. Herein is found the full justification of an immigration and naturalization policy on the part of the United States, which makes a sharp distinction between those races which are widely marked off from the basic American population and those which are closely akin. The principle has been propounded and urged by certain broad-minded and sympathetic persons that there should be no racial discrimination in any American legislation. Nothing could be more unsound, unscientific, or dangerous. Racial discrimination is inherent in biological fact and in human nature. It is unsafe and fallacious to deny in legislation forces which exist in fact. As long as racial feeling exists in the human heart, to ignore it in legislation and policy will be to promote, not peace, but international misunderstanding and war.

There can be no doubt that the founders of America expected it and intended it to be a white man's country, not in the modern anthropological interpretation that would include Hindus and other black-skinned groups in the classification, but in the meaning that was current among intelligent people one hundred and fifty years ago. The calmness with which they closed their eyes to the presence of the Negroes in this white man's country did not alter their intentions any more than it provided an escape from the difficulties involved. There can also be no doubt that if America is to remain a stable nation it must continue a white man's country for an indefinite period to come. We have enough grounds of disunion and disruption without adding the irremediable one of deep racial antagonisms. An exclusion policy toward all non-white groups is wholly defensible in theory and practice, however questionable may have been the immediate means by which this policy has been put into effect at successive periods in our history.

It is highly important to recognize that this is all that is involved in the so-called "Japanese Exclusion Clause" that aroused so much heated controversy during the passage of the Act of 1924, and still acts as an irritant to many persons on both sides of the Pacific. The Chinese had been excluded for over forty years by laws aimed specifically at them. The Hindus had been excluded for many years, first by a rigid interpretation of the general immigration law and later by the famous "geographical delimitation clause" of the law of 1917, which also included practically all the regions of central and southern Asia, and the adjacent islands, except parts of China and Japan. The fact is that in 1924 Japan was practically the only non-white nation in the world which showed disposition to send us considerable numbers of immigrants, which was not definitely prohibited from sending them by some specific piece of legislation. In the place of a law, Japanese immigration was prohibited by the vague understanding negotiated between Secretary Root and Baron Takahira, popularly known as the Gentlemen's Agreement, the terms of which have never been made public. It is generally understood, however, that according to this arrangement Japan undertook voluntarily to refuse passports to all Japanese immigrant laborers to the United States, with certain exceptions.

Such was the situation when in the fall of 1923 Congress prepared to draft a permanent restrictive law. What could have been more logical than that in this law there should have been included a single, concise statement of the principle, already so variously established, that this was to be a white man's country as far as future immigration was concerned? The form that this statement eventually took was a prohibition of immigration to all aliens ineligible to citizenship. This had the effect not only of consolidating the immigration policy, but of making it consistent with the naturalization policy, which had remained unassailed for over a century. Why, then, the uproar on the part of, and in behalf of, Japan? For the simple reason that at the time this law was passed, practically speaking, Japan was the only non-white people not already excluded by United States law, and Japan would have been very glad to keep that status. There was a widespread impression that this law involved some special affront to Japan, and it was widely attacked as discriminatory legislation, singling out Japan for peculiar treatment. The fact is that *the law of 1924 does not put Japan into a class by herself; it takes her out of a class by herself.* It removes Japan from the proud eminence — which she naturally would have been glad to retain — of being the only nation on earth to which the United States conceded any control or authority over the immigration movement, and puts her among the non-white peoples where she belongs. It is not difficult to see that the cause of peace and international understanding in the future was to be promoted much more by terminating such a unique discrimination than by perpetuating it in a permanent immigration law. It may well be true that America displayed unnecessary harshness and unwarranted arrogance in the methods by which the action was taken. It may be granted that there was serious diplomatic blundering on both sides of the Pacific. But there is no doubt as to the soundness of the principle. There are no grounds for interpreting the act as a gratuitous affront to Japan, conveying an implication of inferiority on her part. There is no basis upon which Japan can rest a demand for any alteration of the measure, now it has been enacted, any more than for China's demanding the repeal of the Chinese Exclusion Acts which were the outcome of even more flagrantly indefensible methods. The American nationality is inseparably bound up with white race feeling, and as long as this condition remains an active factor in our national life it can not safely be ignored in national policy.

With the non-white races excluded, race antipathy plays a very minor rôle in the problem of Americanization. The outstanding obstacle to Americanization is national antipathy. It is this that prevents that spontaneous, unconscious intercourse between natives and foreigners by which alone the latter can come to know America. Let it be restated that national antipathy is a perfectly natural, universal, defensible, and on the whole probably beneficial, factor in human experience. It can not be eradicated by an act of the will, and it is nothing to be ashamed of. Like all other natural impulses and sentiments it ought to be subordinated to, and controlled by, the human attributes of the reason and the will. It calls for inhibitions just like every other impulse. But it is quite inevitable that human beings should prefer to associate with those whom they like, and it is perfectly natural that they should like best those who are most like them in essentials. As Dr. A. Myerson has put it, conversely, "The basis of dislike is normally unlikeness."[1] It is therefore inevitable that Americans, without making it a matter of discrimination or deliberate choice, should for the most part associate with other Americans, just as immigrants associate with other immigrants. The heart of the whole Americanization problem, viewed as an enterprise in practical social engineering, lies in the question whether or not it is possible to put forces into operation which will bring Americans and foreigners into natural, unforced association with each other. If every genuine American family were to set up relations of intimate friendship with one foreign family, or even one foreign individual, with no urge of duty and no sense of condescension, the task of Americanization could be dismissed from serious public concern — though in some sections, like the State of Rhode Island, there would be only about half enough American families to go around.

Let the average American ask himself whether the answer to this question is affirmative or negative. The answer of the individual is the answer of the group. Social contacts are, in the last analysis, always personal. Assimilation is an individual phenomenon, not a mass phenomenon. Foreigners can

[1] "The Nervousness of the Jew", *Mental Hygiene*, Jan., 1920, page 66.

not be assimilated in masses, nor can the receiving group devise any effective mass activities which are not the reflection of the characteristics and attitudes of its individual units. This is a hard doctrine. We would like to persuade ourselves that by means of committees, societies, or some other form of group organization we can establish intimate contacts with foreigners which we can not or do not care to establish as individuals. But the truth is otherwise. If John Smith and Tom Brown and Mary Jones are not able individually to receive Tony Sciarini into associations of intimate friendship they will not be able to do so by organizing into a combination. Organizations are, by their very nature, more or less artificial and self-conscious, whereas the contacts by which the foreigner is assimilated are spontaneous and unconscious.

Whatever the answer may be on theoretical grounds, there is certainly no visible evidence of the approach of the social situation which has been described. On the contrary, the native and the foreigner have been, and are, growing steadily farther and farther apart, and the spheres in which they move have been growing more and more distinct and irreconcilable. One reason is that the range of acquaintance today is so wide that one can easily fill up the circle of his close friends with persons whom he distinctly likes, without the necessity of including any one to whom he is not definitely attracted. Indeed, we have not time to really know more than a fraction of those among our acquaintances whose friendship would be a delight to us. Why should we take the pains deliberately to reach out after the friendship of those to whom we are not attracted? This natural process operates at both ends of the assimilation nexus. The foreigner no less than the native limits his close associations to those with whom he feels at home.

The plain truth, which needs to be engraved deeply on the consciousness of every one interested in Americanization, is that assimilation takes place only under certain conditions, that these conditions do not exist in the United States at the present time, and that they can not be created by any deliberate programs devised for the purpose. The barriers to assimilation are found in certain inherent characteristics of human nature, particularly those concerned with group organization. We may, or may not, admire these characteristics. This is of no practical importance as long as they exist. Abraham Lincoln once said, "A universal feeling, whether well or ill-founded, can not be safely disregarded."[1] We can not frame immigration policies on the basis of an imaginary human nature which we might regard as more admirable than that which exists. The only way in which we can escape the evils and dangers of nonassimilation is by reducing the problem to so small a compass that it makes little difference whether assimilation is accomplished in the first generation or not.

[1] N. W. Stephenson, "Lincoln", page 70.

CHAPTER XII

THE DUTY OF AMERICA

THE discussion thus far has rested on the assumption that the importance of national unity is axiomatic. It has been taken for granted that any conditions which threaten the unity of the United States will, by general consent among Americans, be recognized as intolerable. This assumption probably comes close to the truth in the case of the great majority of Americans. But there is a notable body of public thought, all the more influential because it parades under the guise of liberalism, that questions the validity of this axiom. The question is raised whether the United States, in the light of international ethics, has any right to consider only its own national welfare, or whether we are not under a moral obligation to promote the prosperity and well-being of other groups and of their individual members, even at heavy sacrifice to ourselves.

In considering this doctrine we are once more confronted with an impressive illustration of the power of the label or symbol. The words "broad" and "liberal" on the one side, and "narrow" and "illiberal" on the other, have for so long been used to apply to certain positions in the immigration problem that they have become indissolubly connected with those positions. They have virtually become the property of one side in the immigration controversy. If the reader of these lines was told that a certain person held "liberal" views on the immigration question he would understand without hesitation that the person referred to was opposed to restriction, and in favor of keeping the door as wide open as possible. A person with "narrow" views, on the other hand, is assumed to be concerned solely with American interests in a rather selfish way.

This fact places an incalculable handicap on the advocates of restriction or rigid selection. The protagonist who is forced to enter the lists as the champion of an avowed "illiberal" cause has already more than half lost his battle. If he wins, it will be only in the face of stupendous odds. This does not mean in the least that the American people have carefully thought the matter through, and have concluded that a policy of restriction is really a narrow and illiberal policy. Such is not the nature of the label. It simply means that we all spontaneously and intuitively believe in liberality and that the advocates of the open door have succeeded in attaching that particular label to their program so effectively that the average hearer accepts the alliance without reflection.

In our present effort, therefore, to get beneath the label it will be helpful to ask, first of all, what is liberalism and what is a liberal policy and then to consider whether the policy of restriction or of the open door comes closest to the definition.

At first blush one might be tempted to say that liberalism consists in letting everybody do exactly as he pleases to the maximum extent. But on second thought this conception will be discarded, in the realization that such a doctrine more deserves the name "anarchism" than "liberalism." In its place the following may be suggested: Liberalism consists in a desire for the evenest possible distribution of benefits among the largest possible number of persons over the longest possible period of time, and a liberal policy is one that is calculated to produce this result. Such a policy may also fairly be called broad. It is opposed to all favoritism, special privilege, and concentration of advantages.

Now it is so obvious as to be almost a platitude that the residents of the United States enjoy special privileges. They are certainly more favorably situated than the people of any other great nation on earth with reference to their material well-being, and probably also with respect to their political independence, and various other social relationships. The basic stimulus to immigration lies in the desire of persons less fortunately situated to share in these advantages. A policy of restriction makes it impossible for them to do so. It reserves the enjoyment of these unique blessings to those who happen to be established in the country at any particular time, and to their descendants. Is not such a policy, then, on the very face of it, narrow and illiberal? As these words are being written the morning paper brings an announcement of a proposal made by a person who is described as the "organizer of the Liberal Immigration League" to the effect that in the future there shall be no limit to the number of immigrants, though a rigid selection and control is to be exercised.

If the United States is to be thought of as a gigantic pork barrel or plum pudding, and if only the present and the immediate future are to be considered, an excellent case can be made out for this doctrine. Here is an accumulation of good things which Fate has placed in the possession of one hundred and ten million people. The remaining sixteen hundred million of the earth's population would like their share. Very well! let them come and take it, and the smaller the portions into which it is divided the more exactly will the cause of liberalism be served.

It is to reveal the fallacy of just such an interpretation that so much space has been devoted to the exposition of the United States as a nation. The great question of liberalism is: What would be left of the American nation, and what effect would its fate have on the future destiny of mankind, if the natural desire of foreign individuals to share in American advantages were left unrestrained? It has already been suggested that the idea that all immigrants benefit by casting in their lot with the United

THE DUTY OF AMERICA

States is not nearly so well founded on fact as we should like to believe. But for purposes of argument, let it be granted that all immigrants do improve their situation by coming to this country. Does their gain mean a general rise in the average well-being of mankind, not only in the present, but in the generations to come?

The answer to this question depends upon what happens to the United States as a result of their coming, and to the countries of Europe as a result of their leaving.

As far as the United States is concerned, the first and most direct effect of unrestricted immigration is a retardation, if not a definite lowering, of the standard of living of the common people. It is the search for a higher standard of living which, more than anything else, brings the immigrant here. The standard of the American is higher than his. He can raise his by coming. If in the process he lowers the standard of the American that is no concern of his. Nor would this lowering of the American standard, however repugnant to the sentiment of American patriotism, be inconsistent with the principle of liberalism if the final result was an improvement in the general average of comfort of all concerned, native and foreigner alike. If the total gain won by the foreigners more than offset the total loss suffered by the natives, the result would be a more even distribution of benefits wholly consistent with liberalism.

Such, however, is not the case. The nature of the competition between standards of living is such that the lower pulls down the upper much more than it elevates itself. Each successively lower standard that is allowed to enter the competition reduces the level just so much more. The truth has long been recognized by students of the problem, and forcibly expressed by General Francis A. Walker, that the ultimate outcome of unrestricted immigration is a progressive deterioration of the standard until no "difference of *economic level* exists between our population and that of the most degraded communities abroad." Certainly the ideal of liberalism is not to be found in such a dénouement as this.

But what may be expected in the countries of source while this is taking place in the country of destination? Does not the departure of their surplus population so relieve the pressure at home as to produce a compensating improvement in their social and economic situation? The complete answer to this question involves a technical analysis too long and complicated to be introduced here. Suffice it to say that the almost unanimous conclusion of scientific students of the problem is that the kind of exodus represented by ordinary emigration produces no relief whatever in the pressure of population, and may even make it worse. To put it in concrete terms, we could draw off a million Chinamen a year from China for fifty years, or any other length of time, and at the end of the period there would be just as many Chinamen in China as if not one had emigrated. The same principle holds good for any overcrowded country. No such country can hope to find any permanent relief from its problems of overpopulation — whether they be unemployment, pauperism, disease, or anything else — by shipping its excess nationals to a less crowded region.

There can be only one conclusion. The eventual effect of an unrestricted immigration movement, governed only by the economic self-interest of the migrating individuals, must under modern conditions be a progressive depression of the standard of living of mankind as a whole. It is therefore contrary to the liberal spirit, and the label so vigorously exploited, and so confidently flaunted in the face of the American public, is found to have been falsely applied.

But there is more to the question than this. Other interests than the economic call for consideration.

It has been repeatedly stated that the consequence of nonassimilation is the destruction of nationality. This is the central truth of the whole problem of immigration and it cannot be overemphasized. An immigration movement that did not involve nonassimilation might be tolerated, though it might have other evil consequences which would condemn it. But an immigration movement that does involve nonassimilation — like the movement to the United States during the last fifty years at least — is a blow at the very heart of nationality and can not be endured if nationality is conceived to have any value whatsoever. The American nationality has already been compared to a plant. There is, indeed, a striking parallelism between a nation and a noble tree — for instance, one of our own incomparable redwoods — which may be followed a little further, not with any expectation or desire of popularizing a new symbol, but merely for the clarification that it affords.

A nation, like a tree, is a living vital thing. Growth is one of its conditions of life, and when it ceases to grow there is good reason to fear that it is about to decay and die. Every nation, like every tree, belongs to a certain general type, but it is also uniquely individual within that type. Its peculiar form is determined by various forces, some of which are internal and some external. No nation need fear the changes which come as the result of the operation of natural, wholesome internal forces, that is to say, the ideas and activities of its own true members. These forces may, in the course of time, produce a form and character wholly different from the original, just as the mature plant may have an entirely different aspect from the seedling. This is nothing to be dreaded or opposed. No change that represents the natural evolution of internal forces need be dreaded. But there are other forces which originate without which threaten not only the form and character but also the vigor and perhaps the very life of the nation.

THE DUTY OF AMERICA

Some of these are the forcible attacks of other nations, like the crowding of trees upon each other, or the unwholesome influence of alien ideas which may be compared with harsh and uncongenial winds which blow upon trees, dwarfing and distorting them.

Most dangerous of all however, are those foreign forces which, among trees, are represented by minute hostile organisms that make their way into the very tissue of the tree itself and feed upon its life substances, and among nations to alien individuals who are accepted as immigrants and by a process of "boring from within" (in something much more than a mere trade-union sense) sap the very vitality of their host. In so doing the immigrants may be merely following out their natural and defensible impulses without any hostility toward the receiving nation, any more than the parasites upon a tree may be considered to have any hostility to the tree. Nor can the immigrants, any more than the parasites, be expected to foresee that their activities will eventually destroy the very organism upon which they depend for their existence. The simple fact is that they are alien particles, not assimilated, and therefore wholly different from the foreign particles which the tree takes in the form of food, and transforms into cells of its own body.

Herein is found the full justification for a special application of the principles of freedom of speech to aliens differing widely from the interpretation in the case of citizens. This is particularly true with reference to attempts at free speech which take the character of criticisms of the form of government or the processes of the governing agencies. The citizen is presumed to be familiar with the genius and spirit of his own government, and to be sincerely devoted to it. No check should be put upon his criticisms, as long as they are honest and candid. The criticisms of its own citizens are the wholesome internal forces of change in any government, out of which new and more highly developed forms will emerge. But the criticisms and the attacks of the alien may be malicious, and are certain to be ignorant and ill-informed. The alien, just because he is an alien, is not in a position to comprehend the meaning of the various political and social phenomena which he observes about him, he is incapable of interpreting them in the light of their true significance and bearing on the entire scheme of government, and because he has a potential audience of millions equally alien he may do incalculable harm. False doctrines may be infinitely dangerous even though held by those who can not express them in votes.

It actually seems as if each nation developed an immunity to certain ideas, just as the trees in a given locality develop a practical immunity to the pests of their own vicinity. Our own Department of Agriculture is constantly on the alert to prevent the intro-

THE DUTY OF AMERICA

duction of foreign parasites against which our native plants have no effective protection. Numerous cases are on record — one of the most spectacular being the chestnut trees of New England — where a type of plant which from time immemorial had been able to hold its own in its native balance of nature has been devastated if not exterminated by the sudden introduction of a parasite against which it had not developed a means of protection. So in a nation, ideas are constantly circulating which are inherently destructive, but against which the natives have developed an adequate protection so that they produce no serious harm. But the sudden entrance of new ideas or of foreign varieties of old ideas may find the country unprepared to counteract them. The safest way to guard against such a calamity is to reduce to a small figure the number of those newcomers by which such alien ideas may be introduced.

These considerations do not in any measure justify treating the alien as if he had no rights and were not entitled to express himself on any subject, as has sometimes been done by overzealous patriots under the stress of acute national hysteria. But they do justify the exercise of a wholly different type of control over the public utterances of aliens from that imposed upon citizens, and even more the exclusion of those who in the nature of the case are likely to indulge in un-American utterances because they are imbued with un-American ideas.

There are, it should be noted, a few foreigners whose attitude toward the United States is more positively destructive than that of those who simply can not understand America because they are not Americans. Among this number are those, very few altogether, who make it their business to launch direct attacks upon the fundamental form and institutions of the American government. To them the deportation acts may most appropriately be applied. But much more dangerous are those who insolently regard the United States as a mere economic catch basin, to which they have come to get out of it what they can, confessing no obligation to it, recognizing no claim on its part to the preservation of its own identity, displaying no intention to contribute to its development or to remain permanently as a part of it. One type of this group looks forward to a return to the native land as soon as America has been bled of all it has to offer. Another type looks upon America as a sort of no man's land, or every man's land, upon which they can develop a separate group existence along any lines that they see fit. For instance, we are told upon the best of authority that there has already developed in the United States a distinct Polish-American society, which is neither truly Polish nor truly American, but which has a vigorous and distinct character and existence of its own.

More dangerous, however, than any foreign elements, are certain individuals of native birth who in an excess of zeal for the foreigner, emanating, it may be presumed, from a misguided and sentimental though well-meaning reaction from the attitude of ethno-centric superiority so characteristic of many Americans, go to the extreme of denying any merit in American institutions, and ignoring any claim on the part of America to the perpetuation of its peculiar existence. They are ready to throw any and all distinctly American characteristics into the discard if only we can absorb the "dear foreigners" into our midst. They applaud any expression of national pride on the part of a foreigner as an evidence of sturdy and commendable patriotism, but condemn a similar expression on the part of an American as narrow bigotry. A representative of this type, apparently of native extraction, was talking at an Americanization meeting called by a prominent commercial organization in one of our great cities. Working herself up to a fine pitch of emotionalism she finally exclaimed, "The noblest and finest persons I ever knew in my life were newly arrived immigrants, and the meanest, the lowest, the most contemptible were descendants of the old New England stock!" This was the keynote of the meeting, and called forth a tumult of applause.

The central factor in the world organization of the present is nationalism. Strong, self-conscious nationalities are indispensable to the efficient ordering and peaceful promotion of international relations. Every well-developed nationality is a priceless product of social evolution. Each has its peculiar contribution to make to future progress. The destruction of any one would be an irreparable loss to mankind.

Among the nations of the world America stands out unique, and in many ways preëminent. Favored by Nature above all other nations in her physical endowment, favored by history in the character of her people and the type of her institutions, she has a rôle to play in the development of human affairs which no other nation can play. Foremost in this rôle is the development of true democracy. In America the stage is set more favorably than anywhere else for the great drama of the common man. Here if anywhere the conditions are auspicious for the upward movement of the masses. If democracy fails in America, where shall we look for it to succeed? Any program or policy which interferes in the slightest degree with the prosecution of this great enterprise must be condemned as treason to our high destiny. Any yielding to a specious and superficial humanitarianism which threatens the material, political, and social standards of the average American must be branded as a violation of our trust. The highest service of America to mankind is to point the way, to demonstrate the possibilities, to lead onward to the goal of human happiness. Any force that tends to impair our capacity for leadership is a menace to mankind and a flagrant violation of the spirit of liberalism.

Unrestricted immigration was such a force. It was slowly, insidiously, irresistibly eating away the very heart of the United States. What was being melted in the great Melting Pot, losing all form and symmetry, all beauty and character, all nobility and usefulness, was the American nationality itself. Let the justification for checking this force for all time be voiced in the words of two distinguished foreigners. First, Rabbi Joel Blau: "The chief duty that a people owes both itself and the world is reverence for its own soul, the mystic centre of its being." Then, Gustave LeBon: "A preponderating influence of foreigners is a sure solvent of the existence of States. It takes away from a people its most precious possession — its soul."

INDEX

ABBOTT, GRACE, quoted, 161
Acquired characteristics, 27, 42–46
Adaptation, 16–18
  artificial, 34–35
Alpine race, 64, 109–110
America, definition of, 199–203
Americanization,
  means of, 237–238
  obstacles to, 206–210, 226, 238–246
  poster, 179–180
Americanization Movement
  decline of, 165–166
  failure of, 166–197
  origin of, 162–164
Americans, definition of, 202
American's Creed, 170
"America's Making", 166, 215–216
Anglo-Saxon race, 98–99, 123
Antipathy, 57–81
  national, 68, 74–81, 238, 243–246
  racial, 68–74, 105–106, 115, 238–243
Ape, 15–16
Area of characterization, 26, 34
Art, 6
Aryan, 41, 64
Asia, 15, 20
Assimilation, 11–12, 67
  definition of, 136–141
  opposition to, 222–225
  processes of, 228–238
  tests of, 193–196

BALKANS, 151
Balch, Emily G., quoted, 230–231
Barred Zone, 128–129
Bergson, Henri, 27
Biogenetic law, 43
Blau, Joel, quoted, 223–224, 261
Bootleggers, 214–215

"Boring from within", 255
Brabantio, 69
British Isles,
  races in, 94–99
Burroughs, John, quoted, 57

CANADA, church union in, 146
Catch phrase, 3
Celtic, 41, 64, 95
Census,
  United States Bureau of, 89, 146
  of 1790, 89–90, 92
  of 1910, 92
  reports, 92–93
Censorship, 3–6
Character, national, 37–47
  racial, 21, 27–33
Characters, unit, 28–29
Chinese, 240
  Exclusion Acts, 128, 240, 243
Citizenship, inducements to, 178–182
  See also NATURALIZATION
Civilization. *See* CULTURE
Colonial migration, 86–89
  period, 86–87, 100
Colonies, immigrant, 156, 161, 189, 209, 210, 226–227, 234
Committees, 162
Community, 55
Condescension, 176–177, 244
Crosses, biological, 122
Crowell, C. T., quoted, 213–214
Culture, 34–36, 37, 43

DAY, CLARENCE, Jr., quoted, 217
Democracy, 8, 260–261
Dennett, Tyler, quoted, 76
Deportation, 258
Desires, 37–38

INDEX

Determiners, 27, 117
Disillusionment, 230
Dispersion, 23, 33-34
Dixon, Roland B., quoted, 65-66
Drinkwater, John, quoted, 58-59

ECONOMIC MOTIVE, 175
Education, 164-171, 229, 231-237
   adult, 233
Eighteenth Amendment, 213
Eliot, Charles W., quoted, 153-154
English language, 169, 210, 231-233
Englishman, 99, 227
Environment,
   human, 77-78
   physical, 16, 19, 20, 25
   social, 210-211
Essad Pasha, 219
Experts, 4

FAIRCHILD, H. P., quoted, 210-211
Family, 147-148, 235-236
Feeling, racial, 32-33
Figure of speech, 3, 10, 13
Food, 149
Foreigners, 86-87
Foreign language press, 231-232
Franklin, Benjamin, quoted, 88
Free speech, 255-256

GENTLEMEN'S AGREEMENT, 128, 241
Genes, 27
Geographical Delimitation Clause, 128-129, 241
Germans, 63, 101
Germ plasm, 25, 27-29
Giddings, F. H., 57
Goths, 60, 66
Great Plantation, 98
Great War, 11
Greece, 56, 63, 65, 117
Groups, 13-14
Group selection. *See* LAW OF 1924

HALF-BREEDS, 118
Hebrews, 11-112, 223-225
Hellenes, 63
Heredity, 27-28, 117

Hindus, 128, 240
Human species, origin of, 15
Hyphenated Americans, 157

ILLUSION OF THE LABEL, 182
Immigration, 9, 14
   attitude towards, 9-10
   restriction of, 11
      See also LAW OF 1924
   to the United States, 102-106
   records, 103
Indians, American, 38, 97-98, 199-200
Instincts, 37
Internationalism, 247-261
Intermarriage, 114-116
Interpreters, 7-9, 401
Irish, 64
Isolation, 25, 39
Italy, 66

JAPANESE, 63, 79, 128, 240-243
   Exclusion Clause, 240-243

KALLEN, HORACE M., 154
Kellor, Frances, quoted, 160-161
Kultur, 59, 76

LABEL, 9
Language, 38-39
   English. *See* ENGLISH LANGUAGE
   mixing of, 144-145
Laughlin, H. H., quoted, 114
Law of 1924, 93, 112, 132-135, 227-228, 240-243
   of stationary population, 17-18, 24
Leadership, 260
LeBon, Gustave, quoted, 261
Liberalism, 247-261
Lincoln, Abraham, quoted, 246
Lippman, Walter, quoted, 7
Long-barrow men, 95
Loyalty, national, 172-174

MCDOUGALL, WILLIAM, quoted, 44
Malthus, T. R., 88
Man, primitive, 15-17
Mediterranean race, 94-95, 109-110
Melting-Pot (drama), 9

INDEX

Mind, 52
Mixed races, 121
Mongoloid stock, 111
Mongrel, 122, 126
Mongrelization, 124–127, 135
Moral code, 6, 218–219
  codes, mixing of, 147
Mother tongue, 92
Movements of population, 20–21, 23
Mulatto, 115
Myerson, A., quoted, 244

NATION, DEFINED, 52–53
Nationality, 37–56, 140–142
  acquirement of, 42, 197–220
  American, changes in, 204–206
  authority of, 50
  changes in, 63–67
  definition of, 50–56
  influence of, 51–52
  rightness of, 50–56
  traits of, 144–149
  value of, 259–261
Nationalism, 259–261
Nationalization, 44–52, 197–220
  channels of, 46–47
  See also AMERICANIZATION
National origins, 228
  origins plan, 133
  period, 90–93
  traits, 42–46
Naturalization, 182–196
  law, 180–196
  requirements for, 184–192
Natural selection, 27, 122
Negroes, 69, 113–114, 129, 240
New immigration, 107–112, 207–210
Nonassimilation
  effects of, 253–261
  evidences of, 156–160
Nordic race, 43, 96–102, 109–110

OBSTACLES TO AMERICANIZATION
  See AMERICANIZATION, OBSTACLES TO
Oldham, J. H., quoted, 73–74
Old immigration, 103–106, 108, 131, 133
Osborn, Henry F., quoted, 126

Ostrogoths, 66
Othello, 69
Overpopulation, effects of emigration on, 252–253

PALATINATE, 101
Parental influence, 44–45
Parochial schools, 234
Patriotism, 224–225
Pay Envelope Series, 178–179, 208
Percentage plan. *See* QUOTA PLAN
Period of race contact, 35–36
  of race formation, 23–27, 33–34
Population, increase of, 17–18
Population, movements of. *See* MOVEMENTS OF POPULATION
Pound, figure of, 125
Presidential campaign, 3
Pressure of population, 35
  See also OVERPOPULATION
Prohibition, 212–215
Public opinion, 8, 38
Public school system, 170, 233–235

QUOTA PLAN, 131–133

RACE, 13–36
  changes in, 62–63
  defined, 22–23
  in the United States, 82–106, 108–114, 130
  formation, 33
  influence of, 51
  mixture, 37, 35–36, 112–127
    effects of, 116–127
    processes of, 112–116
  prejudice, 68–74
  traits, 42
Racial discrimination, 239–243
Recapitulation, law of, 43
Records of immigration, 86, 90–91
  of emigration, 91
Registration area, 92
Religion, 6, 55–56
  mixing of, 145–147
Residence test, 187–191
Restriction, 248–261. *See also* LAW OF 1924

Rome, 67
Ross, E. A., quoted, 54
Round-barrow men, 95
Russia, 75
Ruyssen, Theodore, quoted, 53–55

SCOTCH IRISH, 98, 100
Second generation, 147, 221
Segregation, 25, 39
Self-interest, 177–181
Sexual attraction, 114–116
Sexual selection, 26–27
Slogan, 3
Social conditions, 187–189
Soviet, 75
Spencer, Herbert, 137
Standardization of the immigrant, 143
Standard of living, 251–253, 260
Steiner, E. A., quoted, 149
Stephenson, N. W., quoted, 246
Stereotypes, 7
Stoddard, Lothrop, 33
Struggle for existence, 17
Sumner, W. G., quoted, 54
Symbolization. *See* SYMBOLS
Symbols, 3–12, 137, 152, 162, 247–261
Sympathy, 57–61
  national, 54–56, 68, 238
  racial, 68, 74, 238

TATAR. *See* TURKI
Traits. *See* CHARACTER
Trevor, John B., quoted, 79
Tree, figure of, 254–256
Turki, 110–111

UNIT CHARACTERS. *See* CHARACTERS, UNIT
Unity, 13, 21, 36, 37, 40, 56, 78–79
  importance of, 247–261
  national, 40, 261

VANDALS, 60
Variation, 19–21
Variety of species, 15, 20–21
Visigoths, 66
Vital statistics, 83, 92
Volstead Act, 213–214

WAIST LINES, 44
Walker, Francis A., quoted, 252
Ward, L. F., quoted, 236
Weaving machine, 151–153
Wells, H. G., quoted, 68, 145
White race, 70–71, 113–114
Will to assimilate, 222
Witnesses, 189–191

ZANGWILL, ISRAEL, 9
Zionist movement, 225

Anti-Movements in America

An Arno Press Collection

Proceedings of the Asiatic Exclusion League, 1907-1913. 1907-1913

Beecher, Edward. **The Papal Conspiracy Exposed.** 1855

Beecher, Lyman. **A Plea For the West.** 1835

Budenz, Louis F. **The Techniques of Communism.** 1954

Burr, Clinton Stoddard. **America's Race Heritage.** 1922

Calhoun, William P[atrick]. **The Caucasian and the Negro in the United States.** 1902

Ministers of the Established Church in Glasgow. **A Course of Lectures On the Jews.** 1840

Dies, Martin. **The Trojan Horse in America.** 1940

Dilling, Elizabeth. **The Red Network.** 1935

East, Edward M. **Mankind At the Crossroads.** 1926

Evans, H[iram] W. **The Rising Storm:** An Analysis of the Growing Conflict Over the Political Dilemma of Roman Catholics in America. 1930

Fairchild, Henry Pratt. **The Melting-Pot Mistake.** 1926

Fulton, Justin D. **The Fight With Rome.** 1889

The Fund for the Republic, Inc. **Digest of the Public Record of Communism in the United States.** 1955

Ghent, W[illiam] J. **The Reds Bring Reaction.** 1923

Grant, Madison. **The Conquest of a Continent.** 1933

Hendrick, Burton J. **The Jews in America.** 1923

Huntington, Ellsworth. **The Character of Races.** 1925

James, Henry Ammon. **Communism in America.** 1879

King, James M. **Facing the Twentieth Century.** 1899

Kirwan (pseudonym of Nicholas Murray). **Letters to the Right Rev. John Hughes, Roman Catholic Bishop of New York.** 1855

Ku Klux Klan. **Papers Read at the Meeting of Grand Dragons Knights at Their First Annual Meeting.** [1923]

McCarthy, Joseph. **McCarthyism: The Fight for America.** 1952

McDougall, William. **Is America Safe for Democracy?** 1921

Monk, Maria. **Awful Disclosures.** 1836

[Morse, Samuel Finley Breese]. **Foreign Conspiracy Against the Liberties of the United States.** 1835

National Americanism Commission of the American Legion, Compiler. **ISMS: A Review of Alien Isms, Revolutionary Communism and Their Active Sympathizers in the United States.** 1937

Nevins, William. **Thoughts on Popery.** 1836

Pope, Or President? Startling Disclosures of Romanism as Revealed by Its Own Writers. 1859

[Priest, Josiah]. **Slavery.** 1843

Reed, Rebecca Theresa. **Six Months in a Convent** and **Supplement.** 1835

Roberts, Kenneth L. **Why Europe Leaves Home.** 1922

Ross, Edward Alsworth. **Standing Room Only?** 1927

Schaack, Michael J. **Anarchy and Anarchists.** 1889

Schultz, Alfred P. **Race or Mongrel.** 1908

Stripling, Robert E. **The Red Plot Against America.** 1949

Tenney, Jack B. **Red Fascism.** 1947

[Timayenis, Telemachus T.] **The Original Mr. Jacobs: A Startling Exposé.** 1888

Wiggam, Albert Edward. **The Fruit of the Family Tree.** 1924

Anti-Catholicism in America, 1841-1851: Three Sermons. 1977

Anti-Semitism in America, 1878-1939. 1977